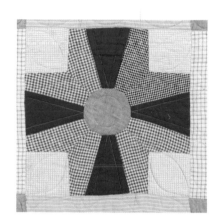

Published by: Kansas City Star Books
1729 Grand Blvd.
Kansas City, Missouri, USA 64108

First edition, first printing
ISBN: 9781935362548

Library of Congress Control Number:
2009924512

Printed in the United States of America by Walsworth Publishing Co., Marceline, Missouri

To order copies, call toll-free 866-834-7467.

www.PickleDish.com
www.PickleDishStore.com

My Stars IV

Patterns from The Kansas City Star • Volume IV

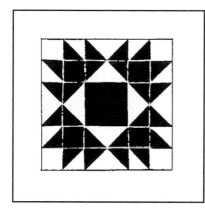
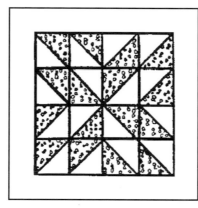

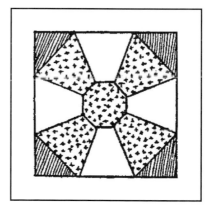
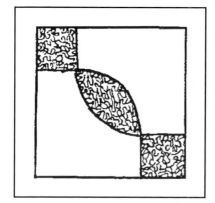
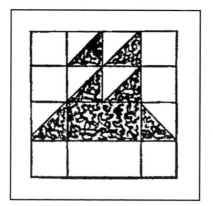

I can not believe we're already to the fourth installment of the *My Stars: Patterns from The Kansas City Star series*. It's true time flies when you're having fun! This volume includes great patterns such as "Pointed Ovals," "Amethyst" and "Rain Drop." There is also a great selection of patterns named specifically for historical events: "Many Roads to the White House," "Red Cross" and "Aircraft." You'll also find places represented in patterns such as "Arkansas Crossroads," "Cheyenne" and "Sailboat Oklahoma." All 25 patterns are inspiring in their uniqueness and place in history.

Be sure to check out the photographs of four gorgeous quilts, including an antique version of "Little Boys Britches" and a new version of "Square Deal." These quilt photos match the patterns in the book, so you'll get to see ways in which actual quilts are made up using the patterns.

The Kansas City Star began printing traditional quilt patterns in 1928. The patterns were a weekly feature in The Star or its sister publications, The Weekly Star and The Star Farmer, from 1928 until the mid-1930s, then less regularly until 1961. By the time the last one ran, more than 1,000 had been published in the papers, which circulated in seven Midwestern states as well as North Carolina, Kentucky and Texas.

The *My Stars* series is Kansas City Star Quilts' effort to redraft the entire historical collection, and offer it in bound printed volumes for the pattern lovers to stitch and collect. Each of the 25 patterns in this book includes fabric requirements, templates and assembly instructions, as well as the original caption that was printed in the newspaper. Sit back and enjoy the heritage of quilting with this fourth installment. The fifth one is right around the corner!

-Diane McLendon, editor

*   *   *

I would like to thank the wonderful team that has made My Star Collection and the *My Stars* series possible: Edie McGinnis, Jenifer Dick, Kim Walsh, Jane Miller, Doug Weaver, Aaron Leimkuehler, Jo Ann Groves, and of course, our quilt friends who have graciously provided their quilts to be included in this book.

-Diane McLendon, editor

*   *   *

My Star Collection is a weekly subscription service where subscribers download a pdf pattern – from The Kansas City Star's historical 1928 to 1961 collection – each week. The subscription is for a year of patterns – 52 in all. For more information or to sign up, visit subscriptions.pickledish.com.

TABLE OF CONTENTS

2) Four Crowns

6) Anna's Choice

8) Amethyst

11) Rain Drop

15) Cups and Saucers

18) Owl Quilt

22) Interlocked Squares

24) Pointed Ovals

26) Signal Lights

30) Arkansas Crossroads

32) Scrap Zigzag

35) Aircraft Quilt

41) Red Cross

44) Garden Maze

48) Cheyenne

52) The Wind Mill

56) Square Deal

60) Beautiful Star

64) Signature Friendship Quilt

68) Cactus Flower

71) Many Roads to the White House

74) Sailboat Oklahoma

77) Chain Quilt

80) Drunkards Trail

84) Little Boy's Britches

Four Crowns

Block Size: 12" finished

Fabric needed

Dark purple

Medium purple

Background

Here's a block for those of you that don't care to use templates.

Cutting Directions

From the background fabric, cut

4 – 2 1/2" squares (template A)

2 – 5 1/4" squares. Cut each square twice on the diagonal or cut 8 triangles using template C.

4 – 2 7/8" squares. Cut each square from corner to corner once on the diagonal or cut 4 triangles using template B.

From the dark purple fabric, cut

2 – 4 7/8" squares. Cut each square from corner to corner once on the diagonal or cut 4 triangles using template D.

From the medium purple fabric, cut

8 – 2 7/8" squares. Cut each square once from corner to corner on the diagonal or cut 16 triangles using template B.

1 – 4 1/2" square (template E)

To Make the Block

1 Sew 4 C background triangles to the center square.

2 Now add the four dark purple triangles to make the center of the block.

3 Make 8 half-square triangle units by sewing a medium purple B triangle to a background B triangle. Set the half-square triangles aside for the moment.

4 Make 4 flying geese units by sewing a medium purple B triangle to either side of a background C triangle as shown.

5 Sew the half-square triangles and the flying geese together as shown. Make four strips.

Four Crowns

6 Sew one strip to one side of the block and one to the other side.

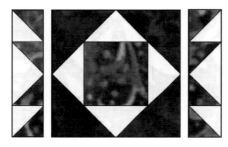

7 Sew a background A square to each end of the remaining two strips.

8 Sew one strip to the top and one to the bottom to complete the block.

From The Kansas City Star, November 18, 1933:

No. 328

Original size – 10"
This charming old pattern usually is made in white and gold but is lovely in any combination of colors. Allow for seams.

History of the Block

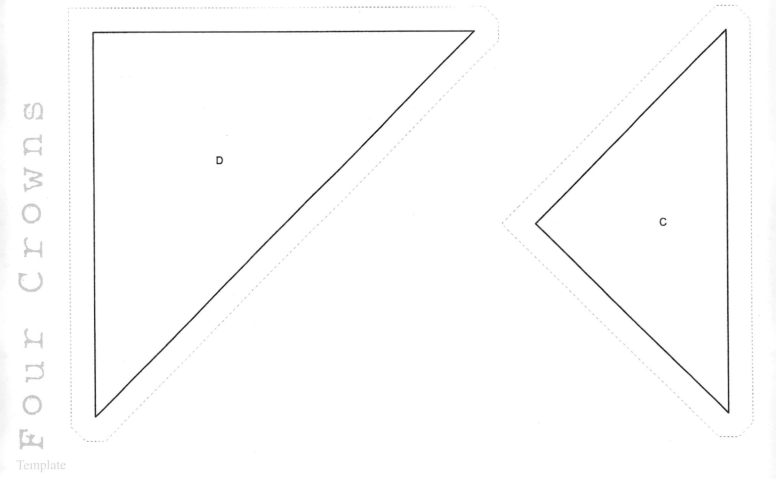

Four Crowns

Template

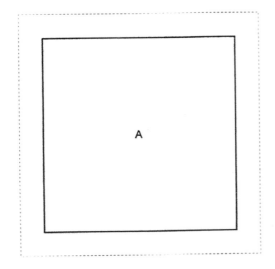

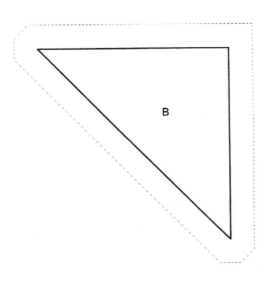

Four Crowns

Anna's Choice

Block Size: 12" finished

Fabric needed

Light

Dark

This block can be made using rotary cutting instructions. Templates are provided for those of you who prefer to use them. I used red and tan but this is a stunning block in any color combination.

Cutting Directions

From the light fabric, cut

8 – 3 7/8" squares or 16 triangles using template A

From the dark fabric, cut

8 – 3 7/8" squares or 16 triangles using template A

To Make the Block

1 Make 16 half-square triangle units. Draw a line from corner to corner on the reverse side of the 3 7/8" light squares. Place a light square atop a dark square with right sides facing. Sew 1/4" on either side of the line. Using your rotary cutter, cut along the drawn line. Open the units and press toward the dark fabric. If you would prefer, you can make your half-square triangles by sewing a light A triangle and a dark A triangle together.

2 Sew 4 C background triangles to the center square.

Sew the rows together to complete the block.

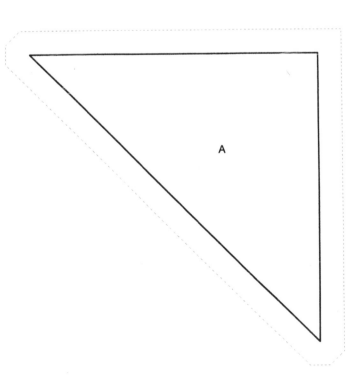

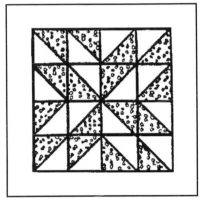

From The Kansas City Star,

February 26, 1941:

No. 640

This very old pattern comes form Mrs. Dayton D. Noel, Unionville, Mo. She prefers the quilt developed in a combination of blue print and solid blue, using a 1-tone blue of the shade predominating in the print. Mrs. Noel started collecting quilt block patterns and designs for homemade articles reproduced in the Weekly Star in 1928 and now has 350 illustrations.

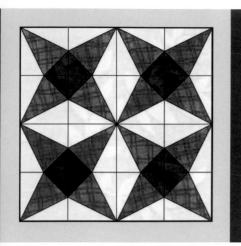

Amethyst

Block Size: 12" finished

Fabric Needed

Background

Medium purple

Dark purple

I've changed this block slightly from the original to eliminate the set-in seams. We will use templates for this block.

Cutting Directions

From the background fabric, cut

16 triangles using template A

16 triangles using template B

From the medium purple fabric, cut

16 triangles using template C

From the dark purple fabric, cut

16 triangles using template D

To Make the Block

1 Sew the dark purple D triangles to the medium purple C triangles. Make 16.

2 Add a background A and B triangle to each C/D unit.

3 Sew the units together as shown to make one-fourth of the block. Make 4.

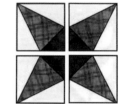

4 Sew the units together to complete the block.

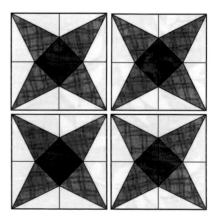

Amethyst

From The Kansas City Star:

February 7, 1931:

No. 156

February is the month of famous birthdays. Lincoln's, Washington's, and among our more recent heroes, Lindbergh! February is also the month of the amethyst, and this quilt is designed especially for those whose birthdays occur in this memorable month. Choose two shades of amethyst, rose, or wisteria with a background of cream or white. Plain blocks fourteen inches square may be alternated with the pieced blocks, or the whole quilt made of the pieced blocks. This pattern is of medium size, but can be made smaller if seams are not allowed. If a lovely coverlet for a chaise lounge or daybed is desired, choose two rich shades of amethyst silk or sateen, with black instead of white for the background, and line with one of the colors. This also makes a pretty pillow top.

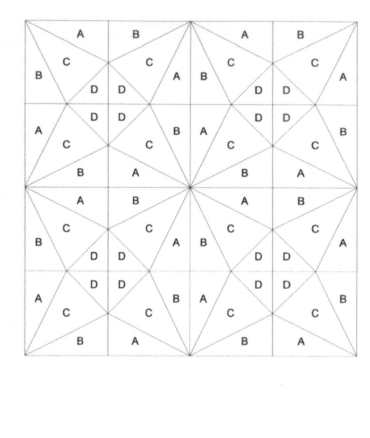

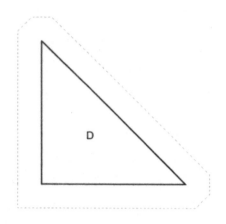

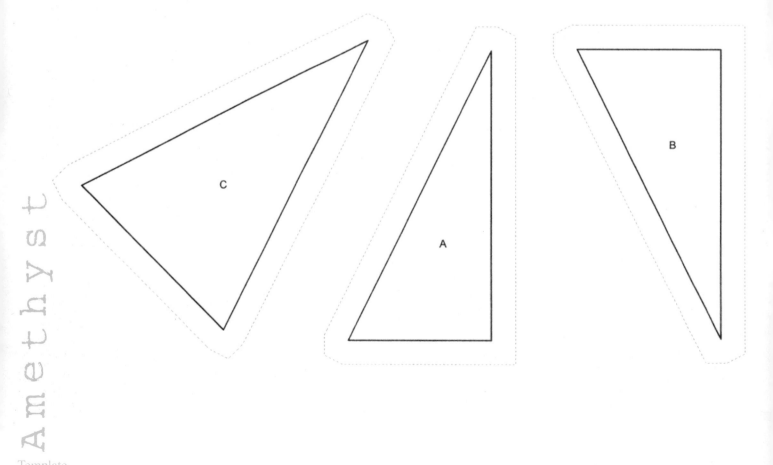

Amethyst

Appeared in The Star **March 16, 1960**

Rain Drop

Block Size: 6" finished

Fabric Needed

Pale blue

Medium blue

We will be using template instructions for this

block because of the curved pieces.

Cutting directions

From the pale blue fabric, cut

2 of Piece B

From the medium blue fabric, cut

1 of Piece C

2 - A Squares

To Make the Block

1

Sew a light blue B piece to the medium C piece.

2

Sew the medium blue A squares to the remaining B piece.

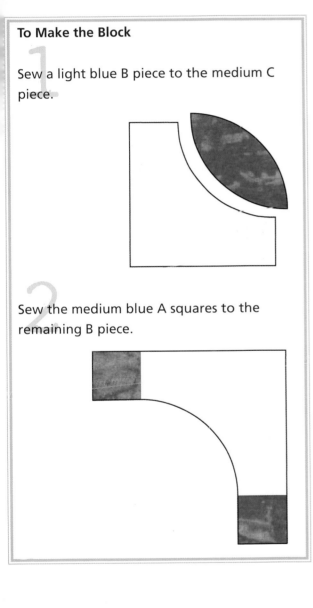

Rain Drop

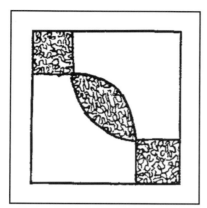

From The Kansas City Star,

March 16, 1960:

No. 1045

A combination of one solid color and three pieces of small print create the Rain Drop. Hazel Mullinax, Farmington, Mo., who offers the pattern, says this is a very easy block to put together.

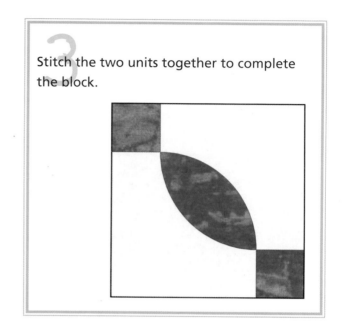

3 Stitch the two units together to complete the block.

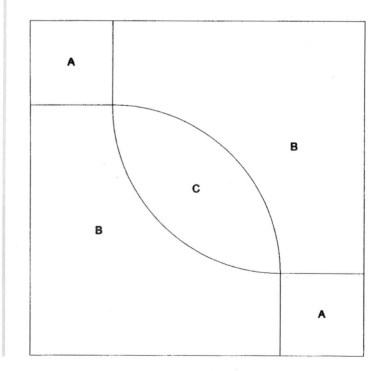

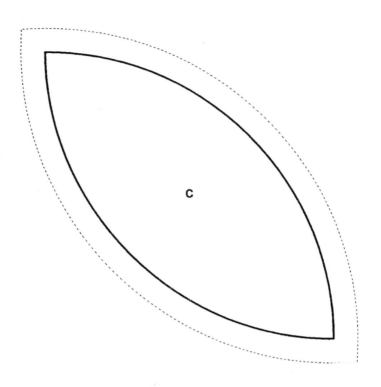

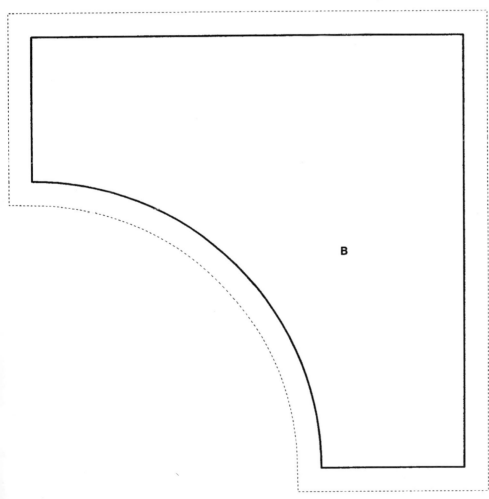

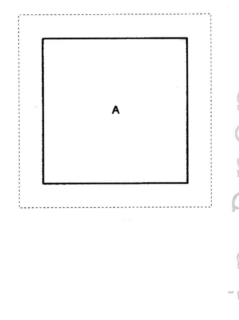

C

B

A

Rain Drop

Template

"Right out of the Blue," designed and stitched by Barbara Dahl, Bellingham Washington. Quilted by Janice Howell, Everson, Wash.

Appeared in The Star **May 23, 1936**

To Make the Block

Make 4 half-square triangle units. Draw a line from corner to corner on the reverse side of the 4 7/8" print squares. Place a print square atop a dark green square with right sides facing. Sew 1/4" on either side of the line. Using your rotary cutter, cut along the line. Open the units and press toward the dark fabric. If you would prefer, you can make your half-square triangles by sewing a print and a green A triangle together.

Make flying geese units by sewing a dark green triangle to either side of a D triangle. Make 8.

Sew 2 flying geese together. Make 4.

Sew a half-square triangle unit to either side of the flying geese units as shown. Make two rows like this.

Cups and Saucers

Block Size: 12" finished

Fabric Needed

Dark green

Print

You can choose to use the rotary cutting instructions or templates for this block.

Cutting Directions

From the print fabric, cut

2 – 5 1/4" squares.

Cut each square from corner to corner twice on the diagonal or cut 8 triangles using template D.

From the dark green fabric, cut

1 – 4 1/2 square (template C)

Cups and Saucers

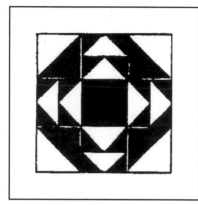

From The Kansas City Star,

May 23, 1936:

No. 456

One of the popular quilt patterns of other days has been revived and contributed to The Star by Mrs. Edward Hendreds, Knox City, Mo. The finished block is 12-1/2 inches square and it may be pieced from solid colors or made from leftover scraps.

5 Sew flying geese to either side of the green square to make the center row.

6 Sew the rows together as shown to complete the block.

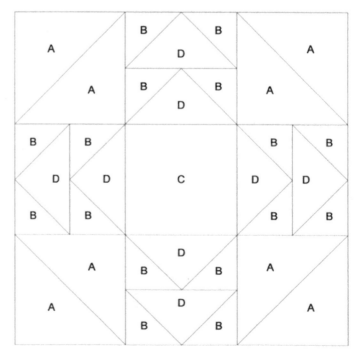

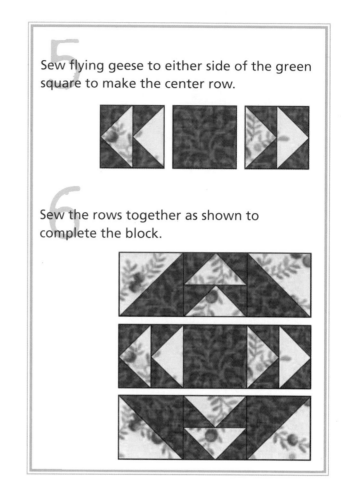

Owl Quilt

Block Size: 12" finished

Fabric Needed

Medium brown plaid

Medium brown print

Dark brown

Background

Cutting Directions

From the dark brown fabric, cut

8 – 2 1/2" squares (template A)

1 square using template C

(This square measures 1 13/16".)

From the background fabric, cut

8 – 2 1/2" squares (template A)

1 – 5 1/4" square. Cut the square from corner to corner twice on the diagonal or use template B to cut 4 triangles.

From the brown plaid fabric, cut

2 pieces using template D

2 – 2 1/2" x 4 1/2" rectangles (template E)

2 – 2 7/8" squares. Cut the squares from corner to corner once on the diagonal or use template F to cut 4 triangles.

From the brown print, cut

2 pieces using template D

2 – 2 1/2" x 4 1/2" rectangles (template E)

2 – 2 7/8" squares. Cut the squares from corner to corner once on the diagonal or use template F to cut 4 triangles..

To Make the Block

1 Sew the dark brown and background 2 1/2" squares into 4 patch units. Make 4.

2 Sew a plaid F triangle to two sides of the background B triangles. Make two of these flying geese units and sew each to a matching rectangle as shown. Repeat using the brown print fabric. Set aside.

3 Make the center of the block by stitching the brown print D pieces to the C square.

4 Now add the plaid D pieces and sew the mitered corners.

5 Sew the 4-patch units to the brown print flying geese/rectangle unit as shown. Make two.

Owl Quilt

Sew the brown plaid flying geese/rectangle units to either side of the center unit.

Sew the three strips together to complete the block.

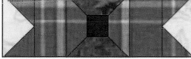

From The Kansas City Star,

May 1, 1937:

No. 501

The quilt, designed for plain colored and print blocks, was contributed by Olive Rone, 13 years old, Elm Springs, Ark.

.

History of the Block

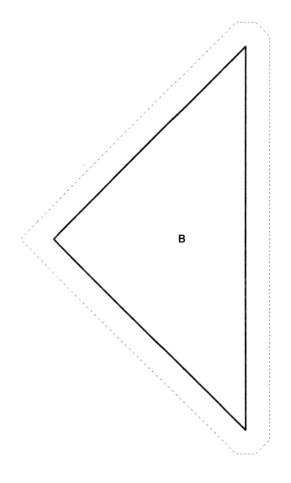

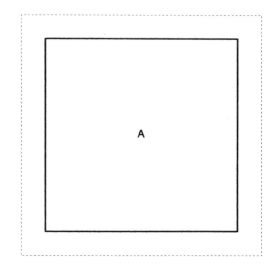

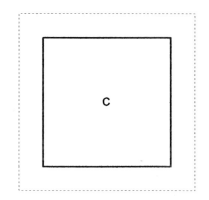

Owl Quilt

Template

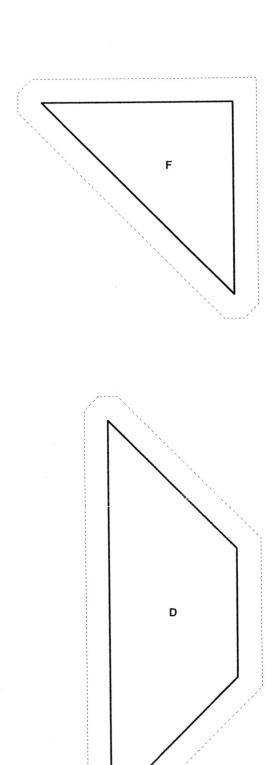

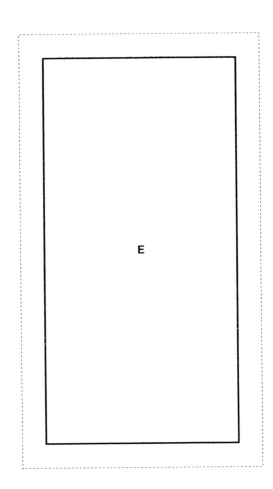

Owl Quilt

Template

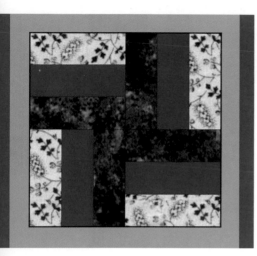

Interlocked Squares

Block Size: 12" finished

Fabric Needed:

Black and white shirting

Red

Mottled black

Cutting Directions

From each of the fabrics, cut,

4 – 2 1/2" x 6 1/2" strips (Template A)

Or cut

1 – 2 1/2" x 27" strip from each color of fabric

To Make the Block

If you cut the 27" long strips, sew them together. Cut the strip you have just made into 4 increments of 6 1/2". (You have 1" extra for straightening purposes.)

Sew the strips sets together as shown to complete the block.

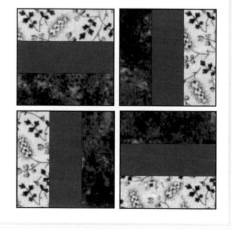

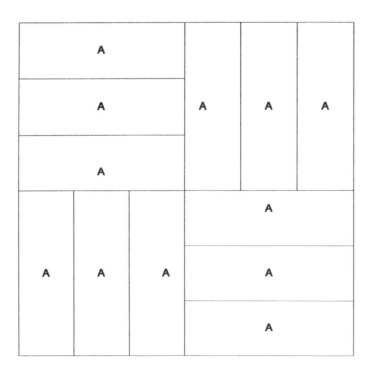

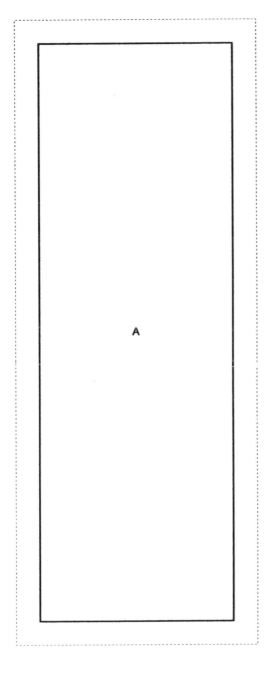

A

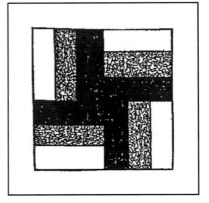

From The Kansas City Star,
September 10, 1932:
No. 259

Here is a puzzle for the experienced quilter, and what a beauty it is when finished if the right colors are chosen! Use colors which contrast well; the center should be plain. The block is twelve inches and alternates with plain ones of the same size. Allow seams.

Pointed Ovals

Block Size: 8" finished

Fabric Needed:

Cream

Light blue

Dark blue

Here's a block for the appliqué enthusiast.

Cutting Directions

From the cream fabric, cut

1 – 8 1/2" square

Before you cut the blue pieces, trace the pattern pieces onto freezer paper.

Press the A and B freezer paper templates onto the light blue fabric.

Press the C and B freezer paper templates onto the dark blue fabric

Cut out all the pieces adding 1/8" – 1/4" seam allowances.

To Make the Block

1 Press or turn your seam allowances over. Then refer to the diagram and appliqué the pieces in place using your favorite method of appliqué.

From The Kansas City Star, April 27, 1955:
No. 950

5 1/2" Pieced. The creator of this design is Mrs. Marie Johnson, Peggs route, Tahlequah, Ok. For her quilt top she chose orchid, yellow and white.

Pointed Ovals

History of the Block

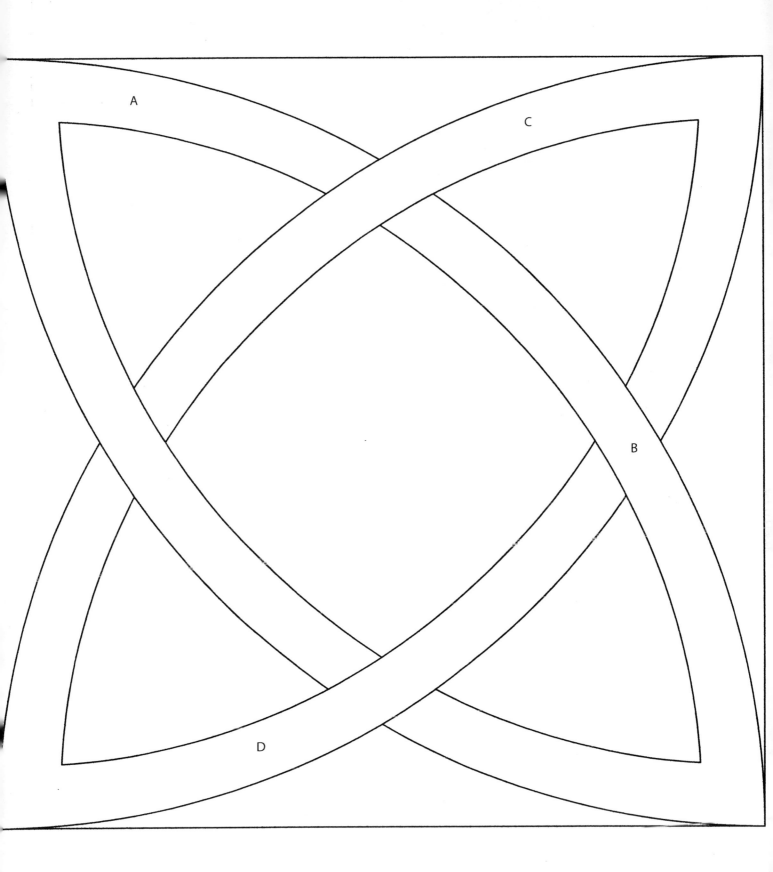

A

C

B

D

Pointed Oval Template

Signal Lights

Block Size: 12" finished

Fabric Needed

Grey

Burgundy

Pink

We'll be using templates for this block because of the shapes that make up the block.

Cutting Directions

From the burgundy fabric, cut

12 triangles using template D

From the pink fabric, cut

4 triangles using template D

1 square using template C

From the grey fabric, cut

4 triangles using template A

4 triangles using template B

To Make the Block

1 Sew a burgundy D triangle to either side of a pink D triangle.

2 Add a burgundy D triangle as shown to complete a star point.

3 Sew a grey A triangle to one side of the star point and a B triangle to the other as shown. Make four units like this.

4 Sew 2 star points to opposite sides of the square.

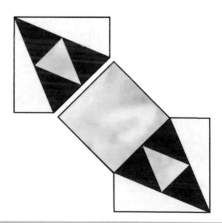

Signal Lights

5 Add the remaining two star points.

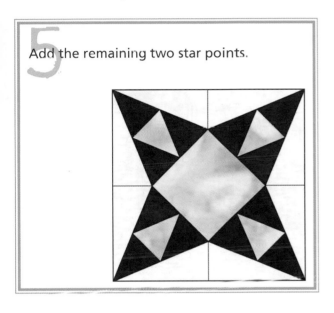

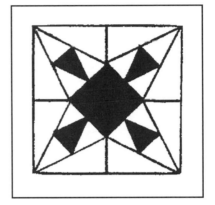

From The Kansas City Star,

June 17, 1942:

No. 690

Enthusiasm over quilt making spurred Mrs. B. R. Troutman, Ottumwa, Ia., to create designs of her own. This pattern is most effective in sharply contrasting light and dark blocks.

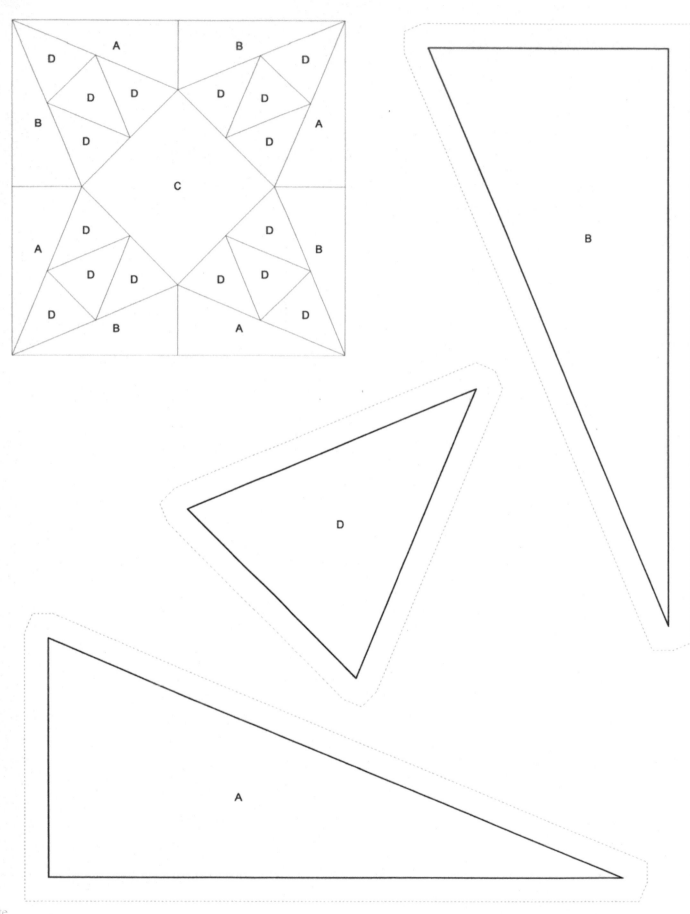

Signal Lights

Template

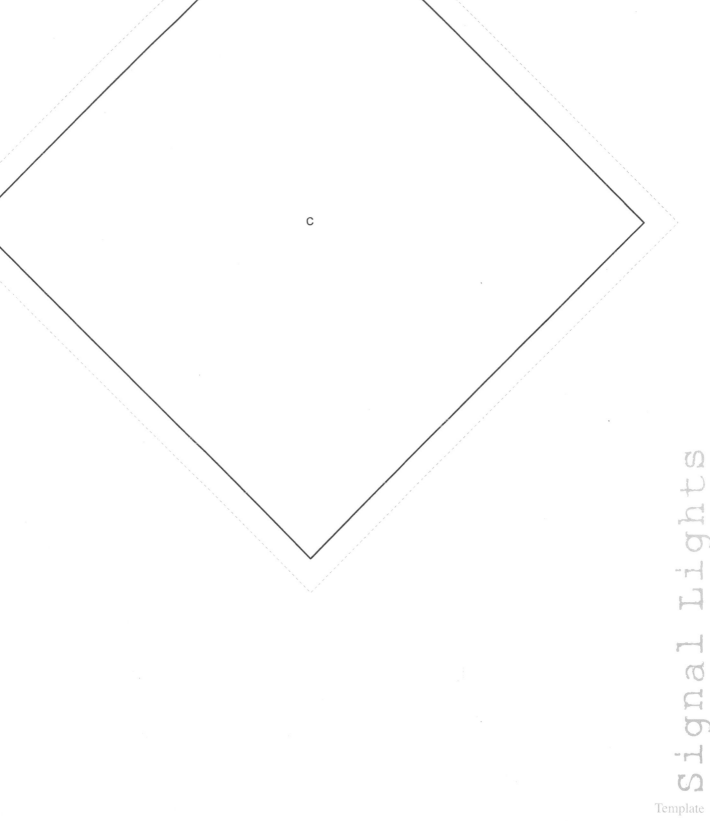

c

Template

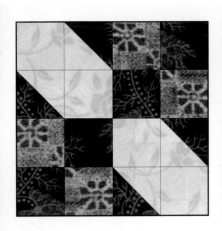

Arkansas Crossroads

Block Size: 12" finished

Fabric Needed:

Light blue

Medium blue

Dark blue

You can choose to rotary cut all of your pieces for this block or use the templates.

Cutting Directions

From the light blue, cut

4 – 3 1/2" squares (template A)

2 – 3 7/8" squares or use template B to cut 4 triangles

From the medium blue, cut

4 – 3 1/2" squares (template A)

From the dark blue, cut

4 – 3 1/2" squares (template A)

2 – 3 7/8" squares or use template B to cut 4 triangles

To Make the Block

1 Make 4 light blue/dark blue half-square triangles. To make half-square triangles, draw a line from corner to corner on the diagonal on the reverse side of the lightest fabric. Place a light square atop a darker square and sew 1/4" on each side of the line. Use your rotary cutter and cut on the line. Open each unit and press toward the darkest fabric. If you would prefer, you can make your half-square triangles by sewing a light blue and a dark blue B triangle together.

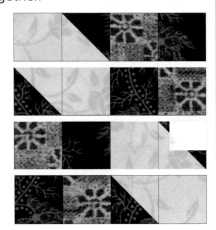

2 Sew the rows together to complete the block.

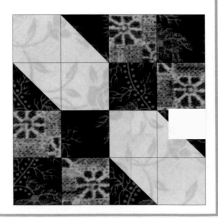

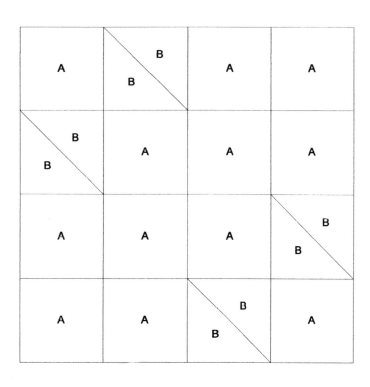

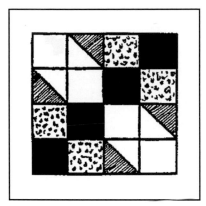

From The Kansas City Star,

March 19, 1941:

No. 642

Original block – 10" pieced. No caption published.

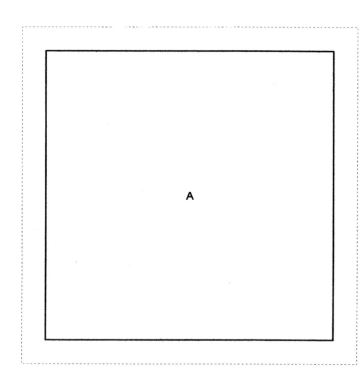

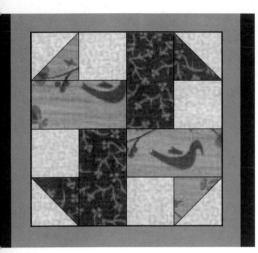

Scrap Zigzag

Block Size: 12" finished

Fabric Needed

Green print

Brown print

Background

You can make this block using the rotary cutting instructions or the templates.

Cutting Directions

From the background fabric, cut

2 – 3 7/8" squares or use template A to cut

4 triangles

4 – 3 1/2" squares (template B)

From the brown print fabric, cut

1 – 3 7/8" square or use template A to

cut 2 triangles

2 – 3 1/2" x 6 1/2" rectangles (template C)

From the green print fabric, cut

1 – 3 7/8" square

2 – 3 1/2" x 6 1/2" rectangles

To Make the Block

1 Make 4 half-square triangle units. Draw a line from corner to corner on the reverse side of the 3 7/8" background squares. Place one background square atop the brown print 3 7/8" square and the other atop the green print square with right sides facing. Sew 1/4" on either side of the line. Using your rotary cutter, cut along the drawn line. Open the units and press toward the dark fabric. If you would prefer, you can make your half-square triangles by sewing a background A triangle to the brown and green

2 Sew each of the half-square triangles to a background square.

3 Sew these units to a rectangle as shown.

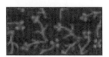 

scrap zigzag

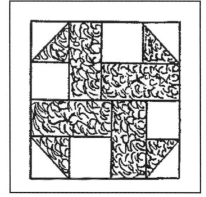

4 Sew the four quadrants together to complete the block.

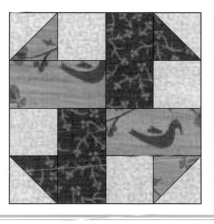

From The Kansas City Star, October 26, 1955:

No. 964

Although the original design of this zigzag calls for a print and a 1-tone, the color scheme could be varied by choosing two 1-tone pieces harmonizing with the print. The pattern comes from Letha McBroom, Huntsville, Ark.

History of the Block

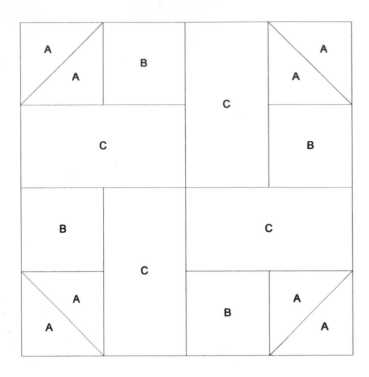

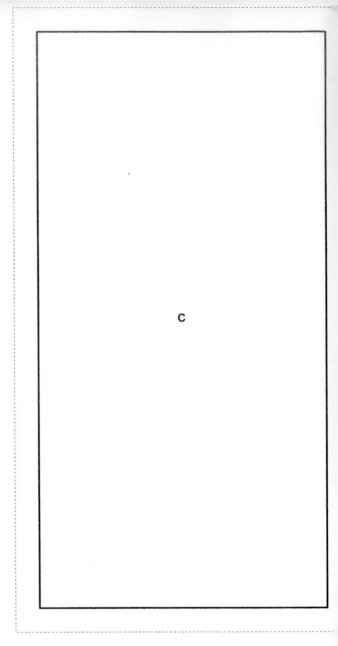

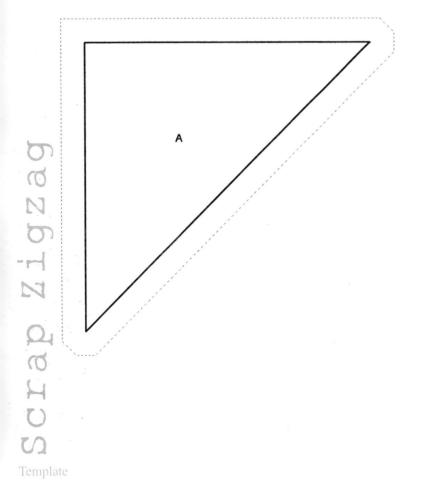

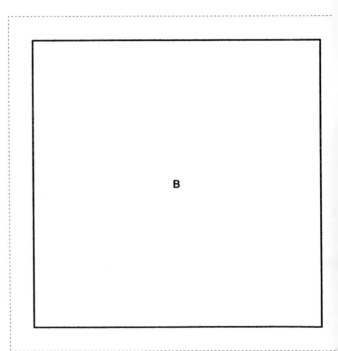

Scrap Zigzag

Template

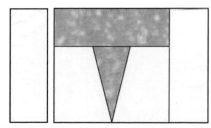

Appeared in The Star **July 13, 1929**

To Make the Block

1 Sew a grey K triangle to the light blue B piece and one to the light blue C piece as shown.

2 Sew the two pieces together then stitch a dark blue square to either end as shown.

3 Sew the light blue H piece to the grey I piece. Add the light blue J piece.

4 Stitch the grey D rectangle on to the top as shown.

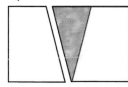

5 Now sew a light blue D rectangle to either side.

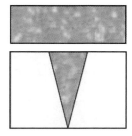

Aircraft Quilt

Block Size: 12" finished

Fabric Needed

Grey

Light blue

Dark blue

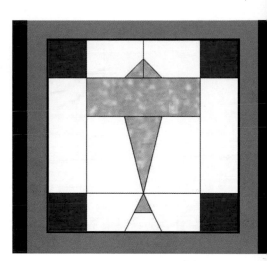

We will use templates for this block.

Cutting Directions

From the grey fabric, cut

1 rectangle using template D

1 triangle using template I

2 triangles using template K

1 triangle using template L

From the light blue fabric, cut

2 rectangles using template D

1 piece using template B

1 piece using template C

1 piece using template H

1 piece using template J

1 piece using template G

1 piece using template E

1 piece using template F

From the dark blue fabric, cut

4 – 2 7/8" squares – template A

Aircraft Quilt

From The Kansas City Star,

July 13, 1929:

No. 43

Here is modern design in pieced quilts. Mrs. Otto Prell, Miami, Ok., sent The Star this design just as two transcontinental airplane lines are being inaugurated in their flight through Kansas City from coast to coast. May it have its place in the history of the world as emblematic of this age, just as our great-grand-mothers designed the saw-tooth and the churn dash and the log cabin patterns which were symbolic of the times in which they lived. Thank you, Mrs. Prell; we are delighted to see this modern motif in quilt blocks. This quilt may be set together in several interesting ways; one is to arrange the planes in V formation, alternating them with plain blocks or in two V formations, one right behind the other, the first plane of the last V just back of the first V. Or the planes may be alternated with plain blocks over the quilt. Dark blue planes set together with a light blue is a suggestion. These single blocks make very nice cushions.

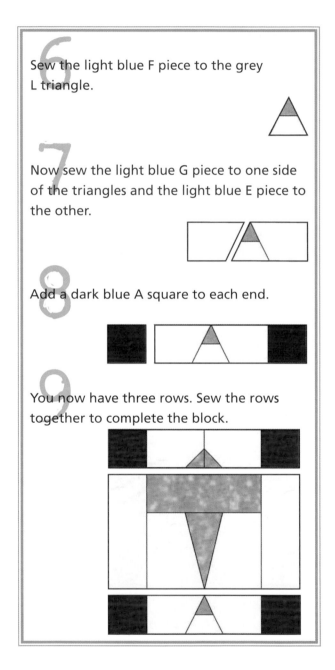

6 Sew the light blue F piece to the grey L triangle.

7 Now sew the light blue G piece to one side of the triangles and the light blue E piece to the other.

8 Add a dark blue A square to each end.

9 You now have three rows. Sew the rows together to complete the block.

Airplanes for Cruz! designed and quilted by Mary Jane Ondrey, Warsaw, Missouri

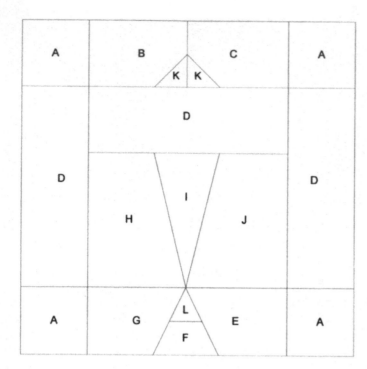

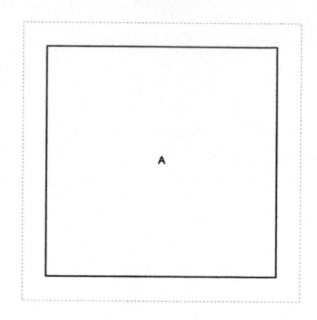

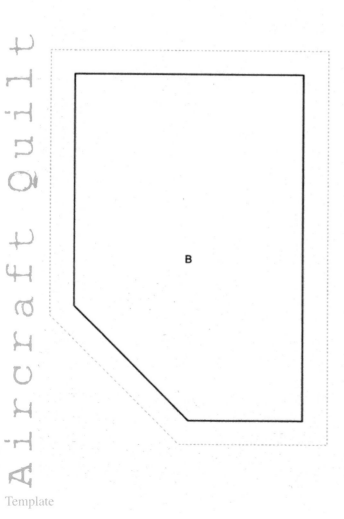

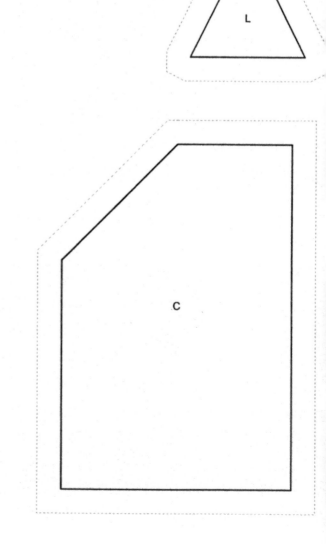

Aircraft Quilt

Template

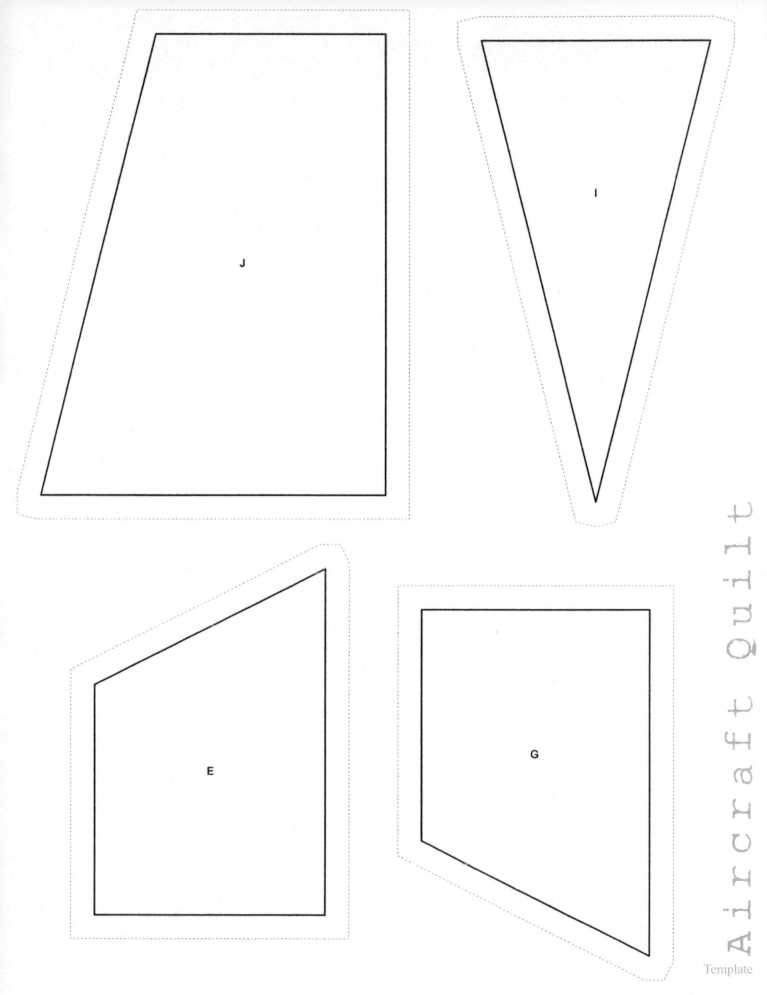

J

I

E

G

Template

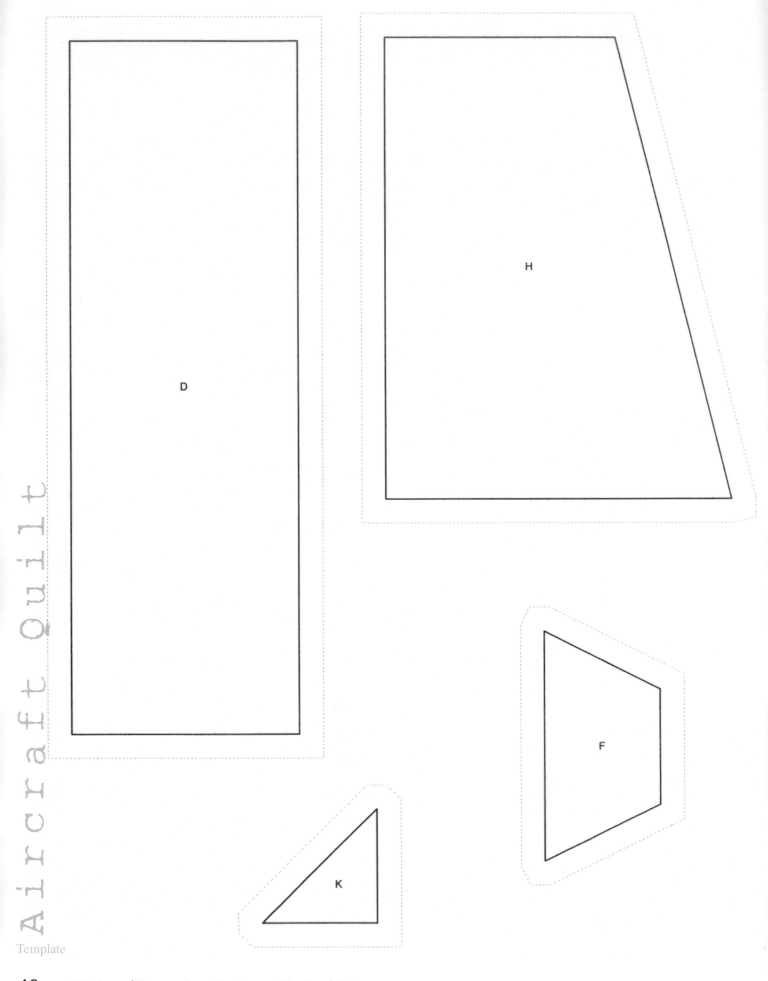

Appeared in The Star **July 21, 1934**

To Make the Block

1

Sew a tan square to either side of a red square. Make 4 rows like this.

2

Sew three red squares together. Make two rows like this.

3

Sew the rows together into 2 sets of three as shown.

4

Complete the block by sewing the large cream 6 1/2" squares and the pieced squares together as shown.

Red Cross

Block Size: 12" finished

Fabric needed:
Tan
Cream
Red

This block was originally intended to honor the Red Cross but you can, of course, use colors of your choice. You can make this block using rotary cutting techniques or the templates.

Cutting Directions

From the tan fabric, cut

8 – 2 1/2" squares (template A)

From the cream fabric, cut

2 – 6 1/2" squares (template B)

From the red fabric, cut

10 – 2 1/2" squares (template A)

Red Cross

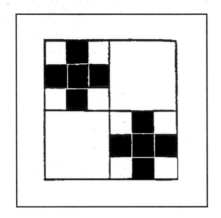

From The Kansas City Star,

July 21, 1934:

No. 363

Original block - 8 1/4" pieced. A Kansas City quilt fan who worked for the Red Cross during the World War knitting and wrapping bandages sent this attractive block which may be done in red and white and set together with white squares which may be quilted with patriotic emblems - the flag, the eagle, the crossed swords, the outline of the Liberty Memorial. Many quilt fans will think of others as they plan the plain blocks.

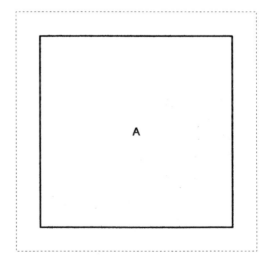

B

Red Cross

Template

Garden Maze

Block Size: 12" finished

Fabric Needed:

Green

Pink

Cream

Pink and green print – this can be a large scale floral if you choose.

NOTE: There are some odd measurements and shapes for many of the pieces in this block so I will be giving template instructions.

Cutting Directions

From the pink, cut

2 – C pieces

4 – A pieces

4 – D pieces

From the green fabric, cut

2 – C pieces

4 – A pieces

4 – D pieces

From the cream fabric, cut

4 – E pieces

16 – B pieces

From the pink and green print, cut

1 – 4 1/2" square (template F)

To Make the Block

1. Sew the green, pink and cream D and E rectangles together as shown. Make 4.

2. Sew a cream B triangle to either side of a green A piece. Make 4.

3. Sew a green/cream AB piece to a pink C piece as shown. Make 2.

4. Sew a cream B triangle to either side of a pink A piece. Make 4.

5. Sew a pink/cream AB piece to a green C piece as shown. Make 2.

6. Sew the corner pieces to a rectangle unit. Make one row like this.

Garden Maze

7 And one row like this.

8 Make the center row by sewing a rectangle unit to either side of the center square.

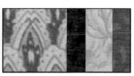

9 Sew the rows together to complete the block.

From The Kansas City Star,

May 28, 1932:

No. 244

Original Size – 12" pieced. This intricate pattern is one of the most beautiful of all the old quilt designs, and a great favorite of our grandmothers. They usually employed two colors, light and dark. A more modern development is to use a single flower center for each 4-inch square, either all alike or all different, then choose a striped or trailing vine effect for the pieces marked rose. The lattice is green. The result is charming. Note that a section of quilt is shown, not a block as this pattern must be a building up of row after row until the desired size is reached. Allow seams.

History of the Block

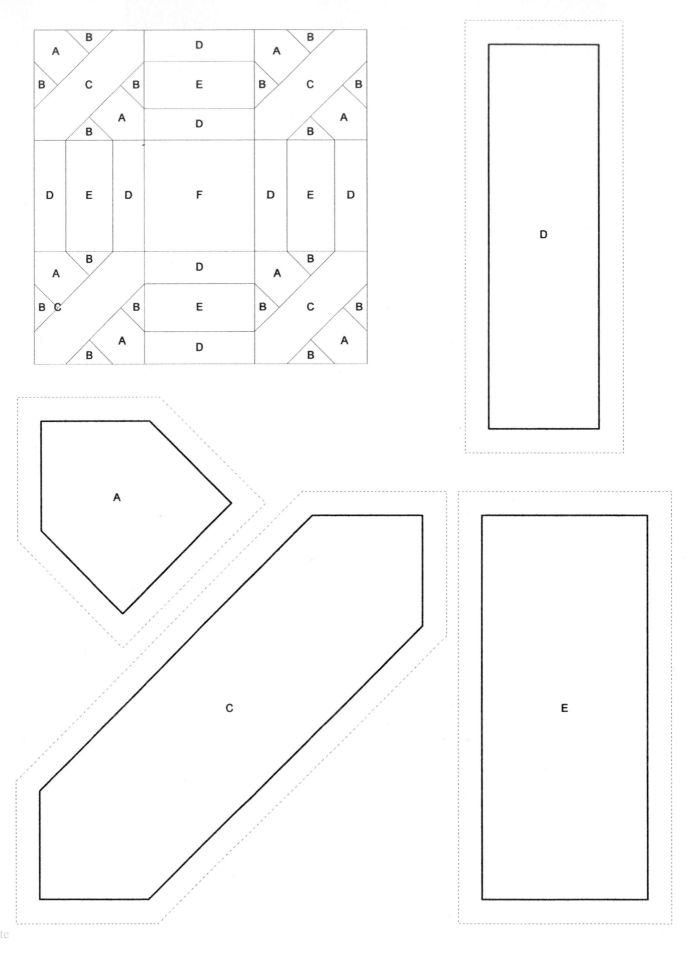

Garden Maze

Template

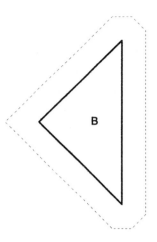

B

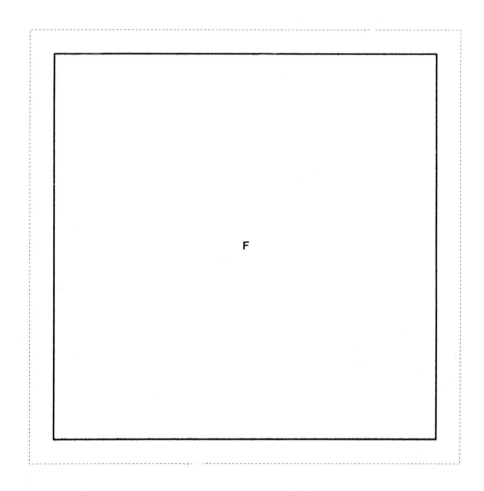

F

Template

Cheyenne

Block Size: 12" finished

Fabric needed:

Cream

Brick red print

Complimentary plaid

This block can be cut and sewn using rotary cutting methods.

Cutting Directions

From the cream fabric, cut

4 – 3 7/8" squares or 8 triangles using template A.

From the brick print, cut

4 – 3 1/2" squares (template B)

1 – 4 3/4" square (template C)

From the plaid fabric, cut

4 – 3 1/2" squares (template B)

To Make the Block

1

You will need to make 4 half-square triangles. Two of the half-square triangles need to be made using the cream and the brick colored fabrics and two use the cream and the plaid.

To make half-square triangles, draw a line from corner to corner on the diagonal on the reverse side of the lightest fabric. Place a light square atop a darker square and sew 1/4" on each side of the line. Use your rotary cutter and cut on the line. Open each unit and press toward the darkest fabric. If you would prefer, you can make your half-square triangles by sewing a cream A triangle

Cut the 2 remaining cream colored 3 7/8" squares from corner to corner once on the diagonal or use the remaining cream A triangles. Sew a triangle to two opposing side of the brick colored 4 3/4" square.

2

Now add the remaining two triangles to complete the center square.

Cheyenne

3 Sew a brick/cream half-square triangle to a plaid square. Add a brick square and finish the row off with a plaid and cream half-square triangle. Make two strips like this.

4 Stitch the remaining brick and plaid squares together into 2 sets of 2.

5 Sew one set of squares to one side of the center unit and the remaining set to the other side.

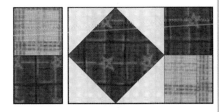

6 Sew the rows together as shown to complete the block.

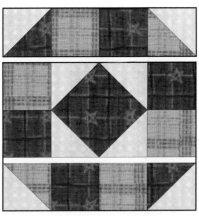

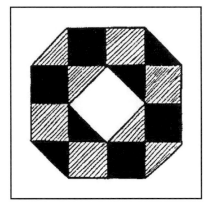

From The Kansas City Star,

September 16, 1933:

No. 323

This block originated in the West when a woman pieced it and named it for the Wyoming town near which she lived. It is lovely in dark rich colors. Allow for seams.

History of the Block

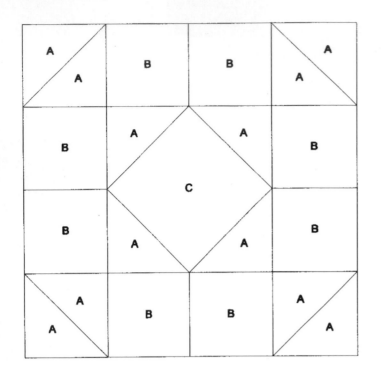

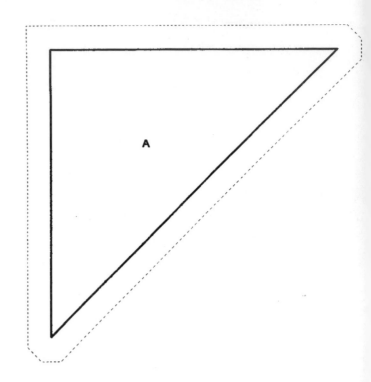

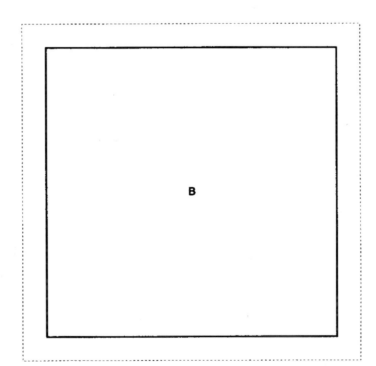

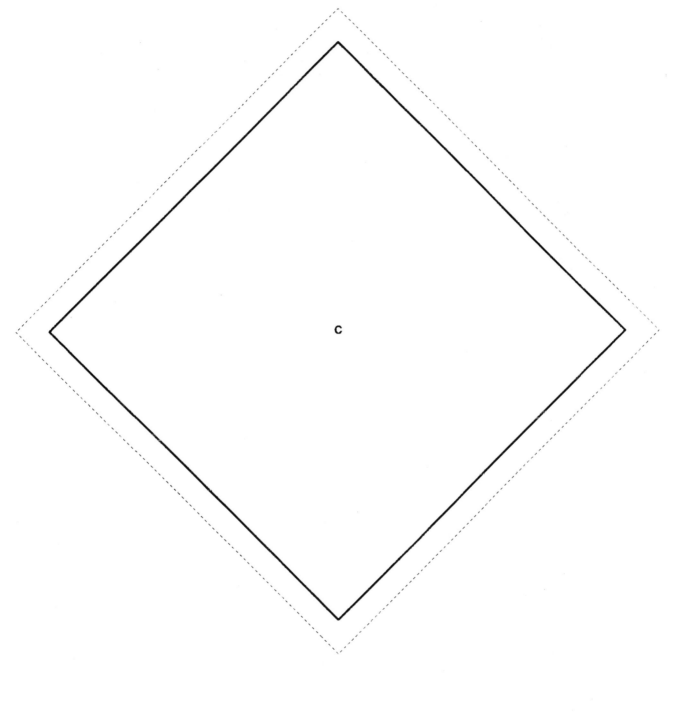

c

Cheyenne

Template

The Wind Mill

Block Size: 12" finished

Fabric Needed:

Cream

Dark blue

Medium blue

Because of the oddly shaped pieces,

we will be using templates for this block.

Cutting Directions

From the cream colored fabric, cut

4 pieces using template B

From the dark blue fabric, cut

4 pieces using template A

From the medium blue fabric, cut

4 pieces using template C

1 piece using template D

To Make the Block

1
Sew the medium blue C pieces to the center octagon.

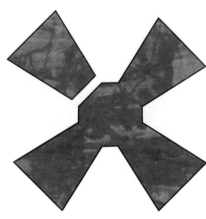

2
Add the cream colored B pieces to the center octagon, sewing only the short seams. Once all the B pieces are sewn to the center, close the seam between each C and B piece.

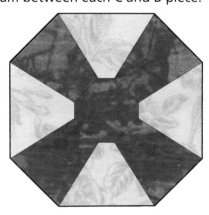

The Wind Mill

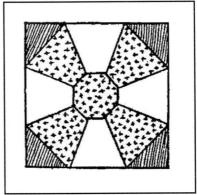

3 Sew the A triangles to the corners to complete the block.

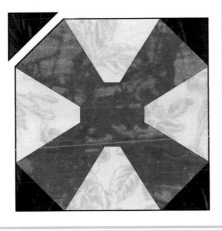

From The Kansas City Star,

August 7, 1935:

No. 413

7 1/2" pieced. Here is a pattern for an all-over quilt or for one of blocks of plain materials. Allow for seams. This block is the gift of an enthusiastic quilt fan, Mrs. Peter Noel, Paris, Ark. Thank you.

History of the Block

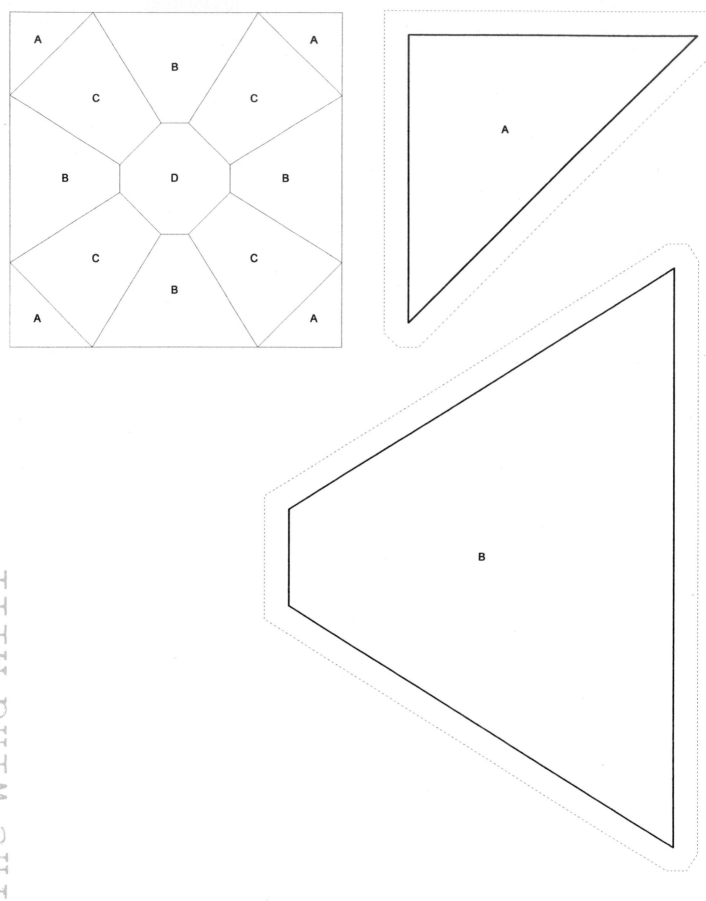

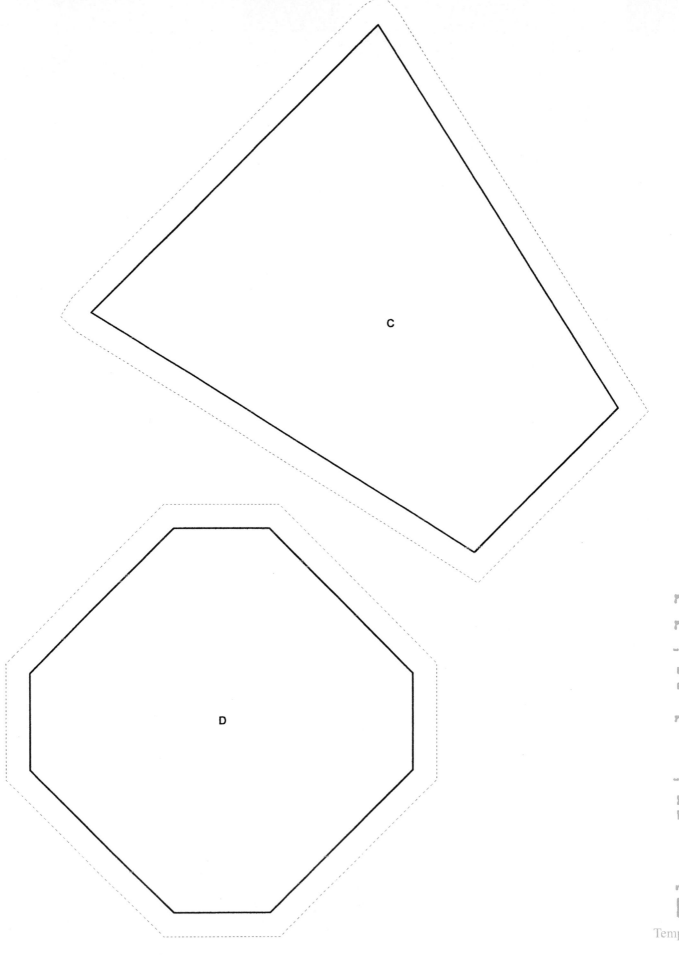

C

D

The Wind Mill

Square Deal
Block Size: 12" finished

Fabric Needed:
Light
Dark

This block can be made using rotary cutting instructions. Templates are provided for those of you who prefer to use them. I used red and tan but this is a stunning block in any color combination.

Cutting Directions
From the light fabric, cut
20 – 2 3/8" squares. Cut each square from corner to corner once on the diagonal or cut 40 triangles using template A.

3 – 4" squares. Cut each square from corner to corner twice on the diagonal to make 12 triangles or cut 12 triangles using template B.

From the dark fabric, cut
30 – 2 3/8" squares. Cut each square from corner to corner once on the diagonal or use template A to cut 60 triangles.
1 – 2 5/8" square (template C)

To Make the Block

1
Make 36 half-square triangle units by sewing a dark A triangle to a tan A triangle. Sew the half-square triangles into rows of 3.

2
Sew the rows together as shown to make the corner units. Make four and set them aside for the moment.

3
Make 12 flying geese units by sewing a red A triangle to either side of a tan B triangle.

4
Sew 3 flying geese together. Make four strips like this.

5
To make the center of the block, sew a tan A triangle to opposite sides of the red C square. Then add a tan A triangle to the remaining two sides.

Square Deal

Now it's time to put the units together.

Sew a corner unit to either side of a flying geese unit as shown. Pay particular attention to the orientation of the half-square triangles. Make two rows like this.

To make the center row, sew a flying geese strip to either side of the center square. Make sure the tan triangles point away from the center as shown.

Sew the rows together to complete the block.

From The Kansas City Star,
August 20, 1932:

No. 256

All quilters will want to add this most intricate looking pattern to their collection when they see how simple it really is. All kinds of tiny pieces may be used, either mixed or keeping to one color. If a smaller size is desired, do not allow for seams, otherwise the block will be 16 inches.

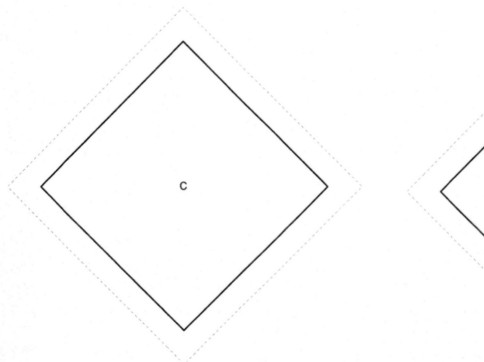

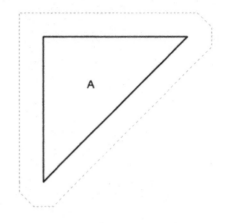

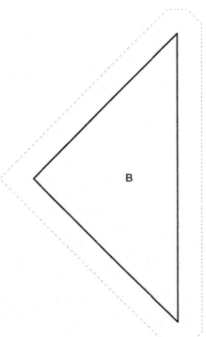

"Srapalicious #2" designed and pieced by Linda M. Thielfoldt, Troy, Mich. Quilted by The Quilted Goose, Troy, Mich.

Beautiful Star

Block Size: 12" finished

Fabric Needed

Light blue

Dark blue

Yellow

We'll be using templates for this block due to the odd shapes.

Cutting Directions

From the light blue fabric, cut

4 pieces using template A

From the dark blue fabric, cut

4 triangles using template C

From the yellow fabric, cut

4 diamonds using template B

To Make the Block

1

Sew a dark blue C triangle to a yellow diamond as shown. Make four.

2

Sew the units together as shown.

2

Add the light blue A units to complete the block.

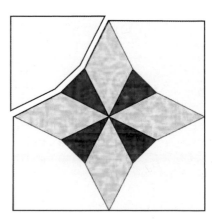

Beautiful Star

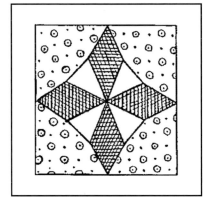

From The Kansas City Star,

March 16, 1929:

No. 26

Variety is unlimited in the field of quilt patterns. That is one secret of their fascination which continues from generation to generation. The beautiful star design is pieced of chintz or calico, which makes part of the block and sets all blocks together. The block itself is ten inches square. When a yellow oil print combines with dull red and unbleached muslin in the blcoks it makes a coverlet well worth making. Or the "star" may be made in a pale green plain material and set on a background of green print.

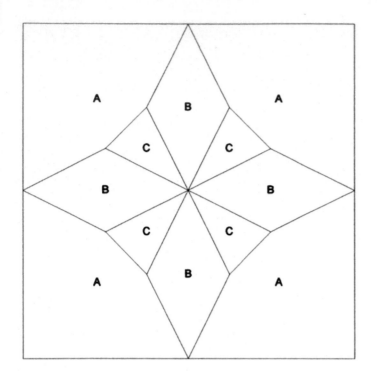

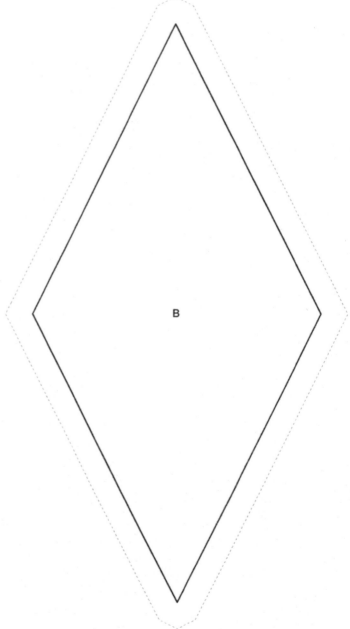

B

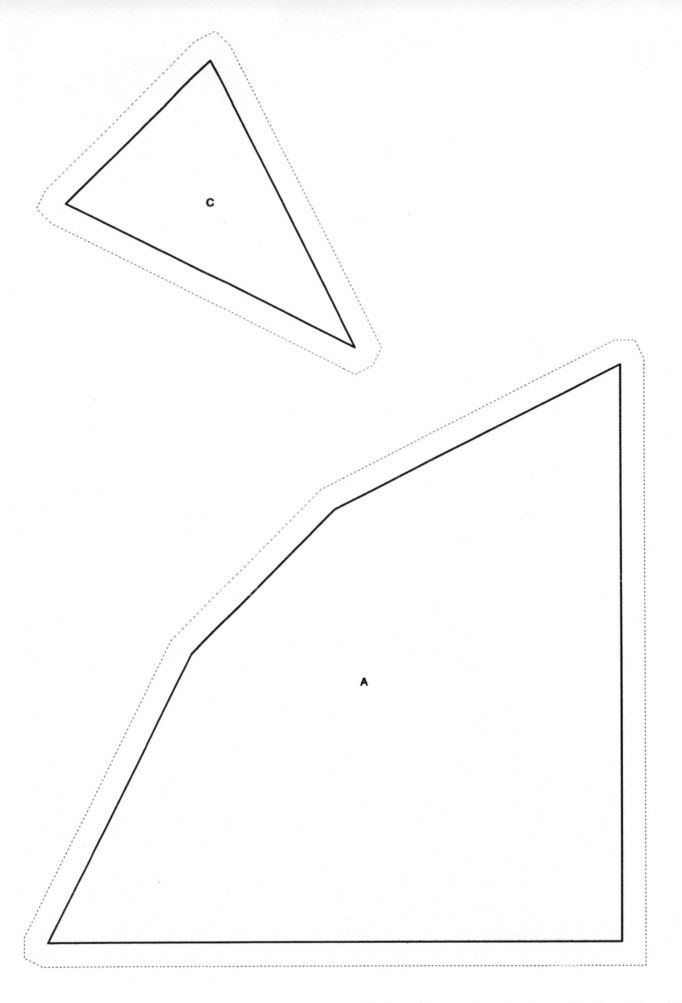

C

A

Beautiful Star

Signature Friendship Quilt

Block Size: 12" finished

Fabric Needed

Cream

Medium blue

Dark blue

You will be able to cut out every piece without using a template except for the center strip.

Cutting Directions

From the dark blue fabric, cut

4 – 3 1/2" squares (template A)

1 – 7 1/4" square. Cut the square from corner to corner twice on the diagonal or cut 4 triangles using template E.

From the medium blue fabric, cut

1 - 5 3/8" square. Cut the square from corner to corner once on the diagonal or cut two triangles using template C.

From the cream colored fabric, cut

1 – piece using template D

4 – 3 7/8" squares. Cut each square once on the diagonal or cut 8 triangles using template B.

To Make the Block

1 Sew the cream colored B triangles to the dark blue E triangles. Make 4 of these flying geese units.

2 Sew the medium blue C triangles to piece D.

3 Sew a dark blue A square to each end of two of the flying geese as shown.

4 Sew a flying geese unit to either side of the C/D square.

Signature Friendship Quilt

You should now have three strips. Sew the strips together as shown to complete the block.

From The Kansas City Star, June 17, 1953:

No. 924

Original size – 10"

Whether you like a name quilt for its sentimentality, or are in a money-making state of mind on behalf of a club, here is a design offering space for nine signatures in each square. Mrs. Ed Draper, Orlando, Ok., creator of the design, prefers the same color for all the 1-tone pieces.

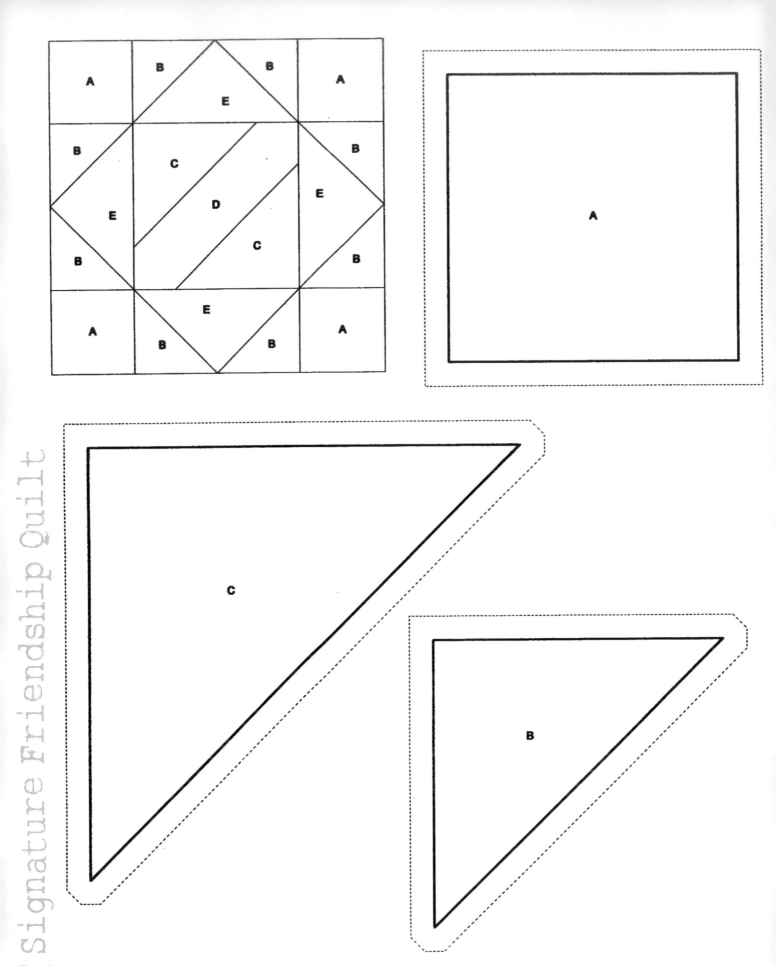

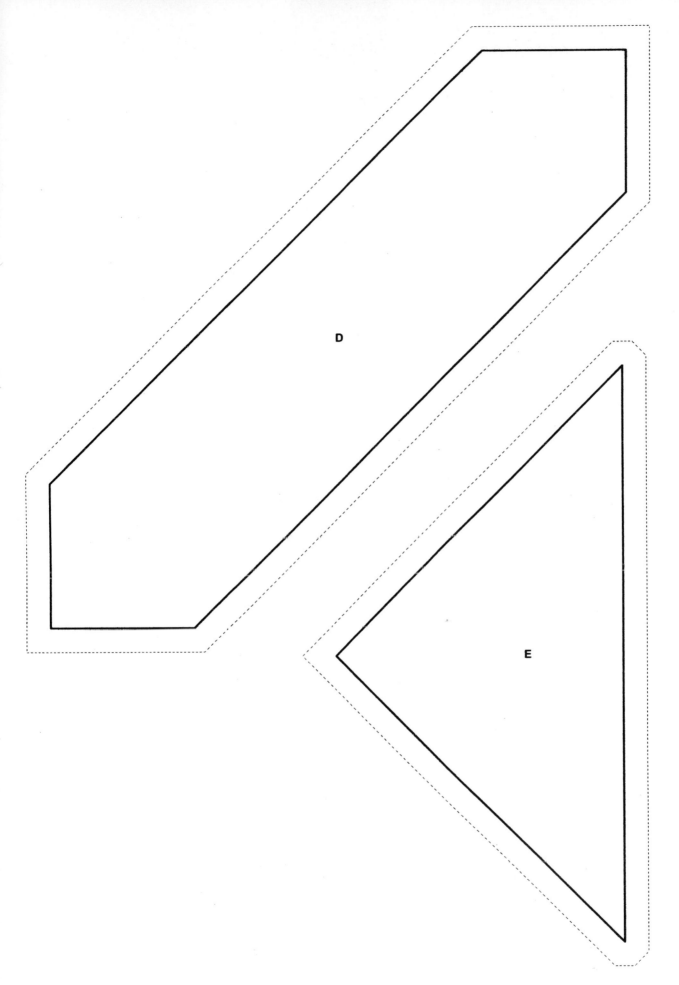

D

E

Template

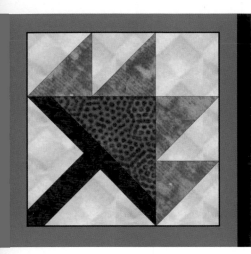

Cactus Flower

Block Size: 6" finished

Fabric Needed:

Cream

Light peach

Dark peach

Green

Much of this block can be cut using the rotary cutter but you'll need templates for the rest.

Cutting Directions

From the light peach fabric, cut

2 – 2 7/8" squares or 4 triangles using template A

From the dark peach fabric, cut

1 - 4 1/8" square. Cut the square once from corner to corner on the diagonal or cut the triangle using template F.

From the cream colored fabric, cut

2 – 2 7/8" squares or 4 triangles using template A

1 – 2 1/2" square (template B)

1 – 4 3/4" square. Cut the square twice on the diagonal or use template C and cut 2 triangles.

From the green fabric, cut

1 piece using template E

1 piece using template D

To Make the Block

1 You need to make 4 peach and cream half-square triangles. If you cut triangles using template A, sew the peach and cream triangles together. If you cut squares, use the following instructions.

To make half-square triangles, draw a line from corner to corner on the diagonal on the reverse side of the lightest fabric. Place a light square atop a darker square and sew 1/4" on each side of the line. Use your rotary cutter and cut on the line. Open each unit and press toward the darkest fabric.

Sew the green E piece to the dark peach F triangle.

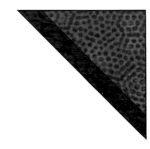

2 Sew the two cream C triangles to either side of the green D piece.

Cactus Flower

3

Stitch the C/D/C unit to the F/E unit.

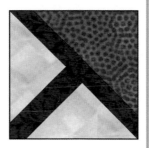

4

Sew two half-square triangle units together. Then sew them to the C/D/E/F unit as shown.

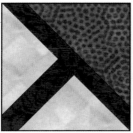

5

Sew two half-square triangle units to the cream B square.

6

Complete the block by stitching the top row on as shown.

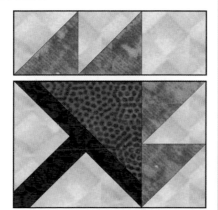

From The Kansas City Star,

July 4, 1931:

No. 177

Original size – 12" pieced. There are several ways of setting together this interesting variation of the old Maple Leaf motif. Use plain 6-inch squares, the size of the block and set together diagonally with the flower standing straight up, or consider this block as one of four, making a block 12 inches with the stems pointing inward, then set together in straight rows, alternating with 12-inch plain blocks. If desired the stem may be slightly curved, instead of being straight. The strip and stem, indicated by the dotted line on the 4-inch square, should be on the bias and are appliqued onto the square. Either plain or figured fabric may be used. No seams allowed.

History of the Block

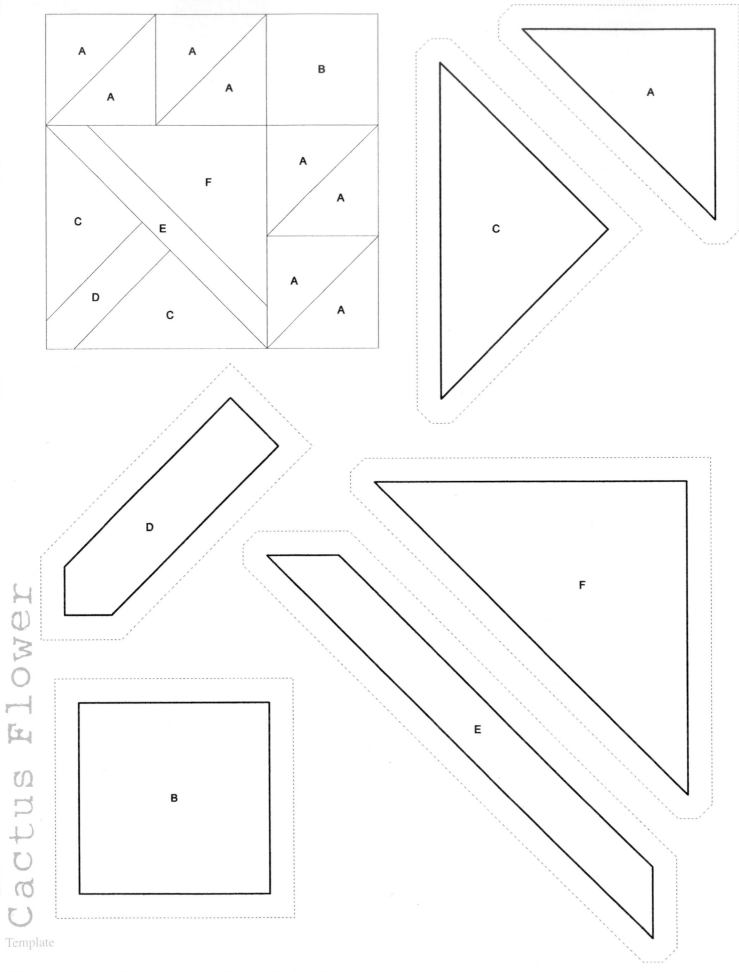

Cactus Flower

Template

Appeared in The Star **August 17, 1955**

**Many Roads to the
White House**

Block Size: 12" finished

Fabric Needed:

Cream

Brown print

Tan

To Make the Block

1 Sew a cream C piece to a brown print B piece. Make 8.

2 Sew a BC unit to both sides of a tan A piece. Make 4.

3 Sew the 4 quadrants of the block together as shown.

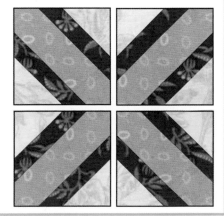

For this block we will use templates because of the odd shape of two of the pieces.

Cutting Directions

From the cream fabric, cut

8 triangles using template C

From the brown print, cut

8 pieces using template B

From the tan fabric, cut

4 pieces using template A

Many Roads to the White House

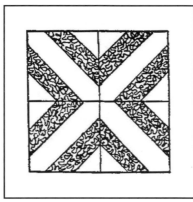

From The Kansas City Star,

August 17, 1955:

No. 957

Original block – 17" pieced. Easy to piece and offering an unlimited choice of combinations in 1-tone and print pieces is this design coming from Mrs. Millie Kolling, route 2, Chapman, Kas.

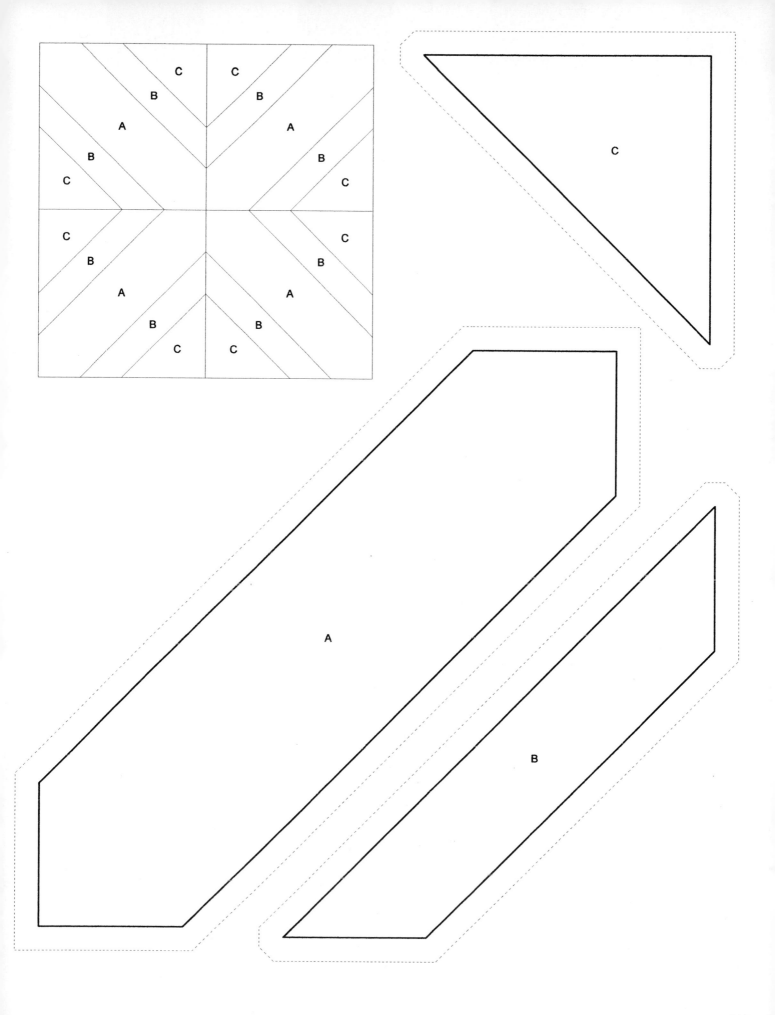

Sailboat Oklahoma

Block Size: 12" finished

Fabric Needed

Light blue

Cream

Dark green

Medium blue

Cutting Directions

From the light blue, cut

4 – 3 1/2" squares (template A)

2 – 3 7/8" squares or 4 triangles using

template B

From the cream, cut

2 – 3 7/8" squares or 4 triangles using

template B

From the dark green, cut

2 – 3 1/2" squares (template A)

1 – 3 7/8" square or two triangles using

template B

From the medium blue, cut

4 – 3 1/2" squares (template A)

1 – 3 7/8" square or 2 triangles using template B

To Make the Block

You will need to make half-square triangles for this block. To make half-square triangles, draw a line from corner to corner on the diagonal on the reverse side of the lightest fabric. Place a light square atop a darker square and sew 1/4" on each side of the line. Use your rotary cutter and cut on the line. Open each unit and press toward the darkest fabric.

If you are using triangles cut using template B, sew the light triangles to the darker triangles.

You will need the following half-square triangles:
4 – cream and light blue
2 – dark green and medium blue

Sew a light blue square to a light blue/cream half-square triangle. Add another light blue/cream half-square triangle and end with a light blue square. Make two strips like this.

Sailboat Oklahoma

2 Sew the two green 3 1/2" squares together. Sew a blue/green half-square triangle to either side. Make one strip.

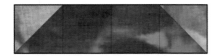

3 Sew the four medium blue squares together. This is the final strip for this block.

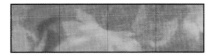

4 Sew the two green 3 1/2" squares together. Sew a blue/green half-square triangle to either side. Make one strip.

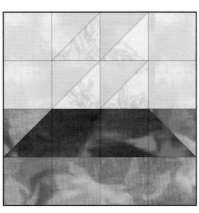

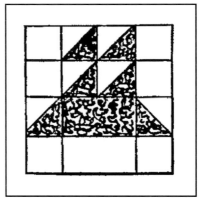

From The Kansas City Star,

June 28, 1944:

No. 746

Lovers of the sea will enjoy this small watercraft design. It comes from Mrs. J. R. Barnes, Williams, Ok.

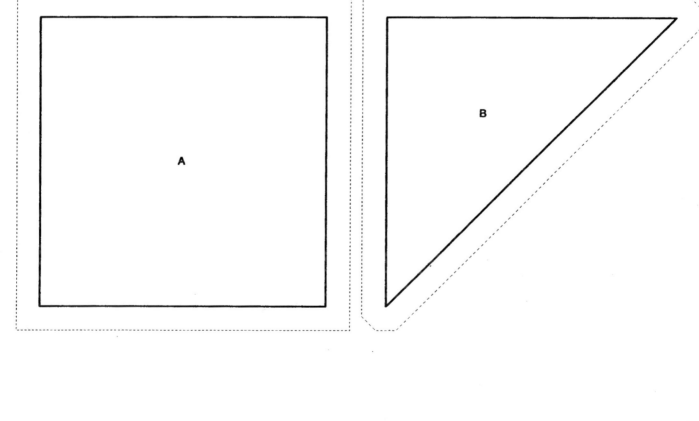

Template

Appeared in The Star **February 25, 1942**

Chain Quilt

Block Size: 12" finished

Fabric Needed:

Scraps of various shades

of blue

Cream

We'll be using templates

for this block since it consists

of curved pieces.

To Make the Block

1 Fold each A and each B piece in half and finger press a crease at the halfway point.

Pin the blue B pieces to the cream A pieces. Begin by matching up the center creases, then match up the ends. Pin the pieces closely around the curve, then stitch in place. Make 9 AB units per block.

2 Sew the units into rows of three.

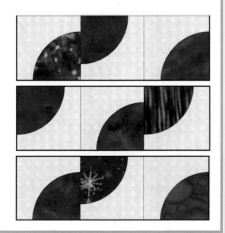

Cutting Directions

From the cream fabric, cut

9 pieces using template A

From the blue scraps, cut

9 pieces using template B

Chain Quilt

From The Kansas City Star,

February 25, 1942:

No. 679

Original size – 9 3/4" pieced. Mrs. A. Matushek, R. R. 3, Cuba, Mo., contributor of the Chain Quilt pattern, says each row of chains should be worked in one color throughout the quilt. She completed a quilt done in five pastel shades - rose, orchid, yellow, pink and green broadcloth, set in white broadcloth.

3 Sew the rows together to complete the block.

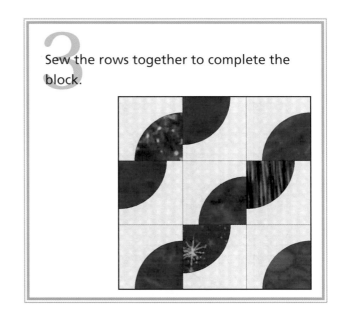

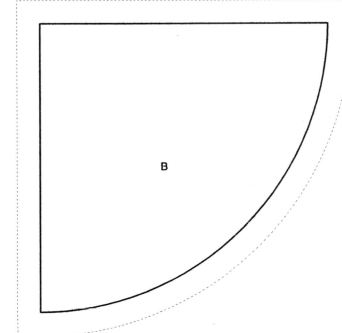

Chain Quilt

Template

Drunkard's Trail

Block Size: 6" finished

Fabric needed:

Light blue

Medium blue

Assorted scraps or

striped fabric

We'll be using templates for this block because of the curved elements. For the center of piece C you can use scraps or striped fabric.

Cutting Directions

From the light blue fabric, cut

2 pieces using template A

From the medium blue fabric, cut

2 pieces using template B

From the striped fabric or sewn scraps, cut

1 piece using template C

To Make the Block

1

If you are using scraps for piece C, sew together enough 1 1/2" – 1 3/4" strips that you can cut out the necessary piece.

Sew a medium blue piece to each A piece. You'll have two pieces that look like this.

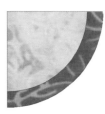

2

Sew each AB unit to the C piece to complete the block.

Drunkard's Trail

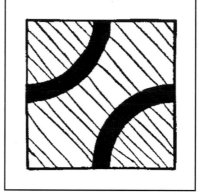

From The Kansas City Star,

September 16, 1942:

No. 698

Original block – 9" pieced. This wavering design comes from Miss Pauline Drawbaugh, R. R. 1, Arkinda, Ark.

History of the Block

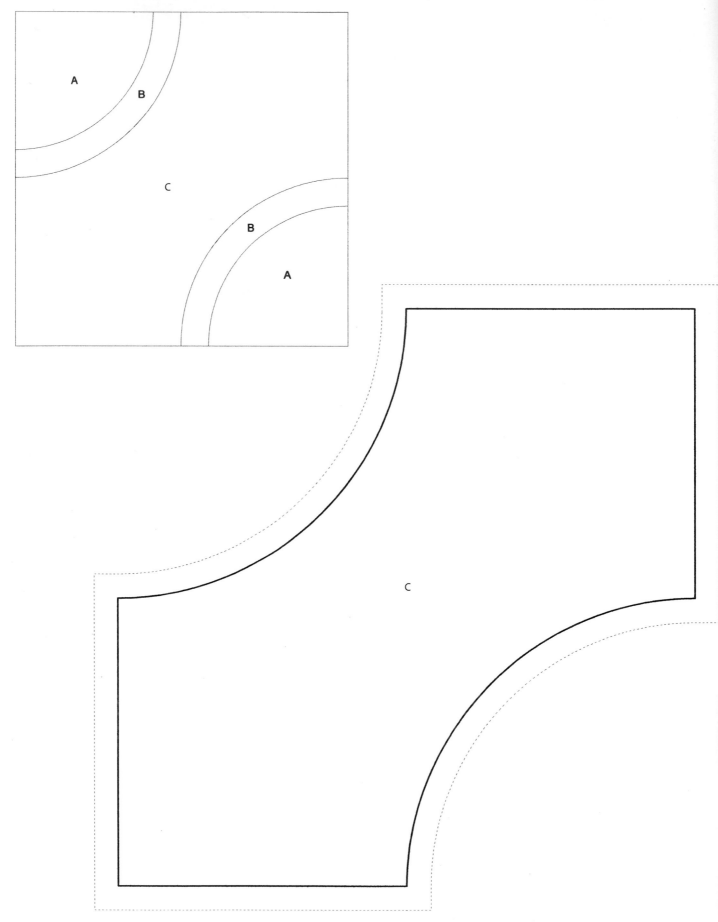

Drunkard's Trail

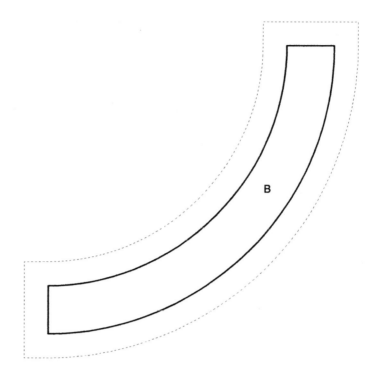

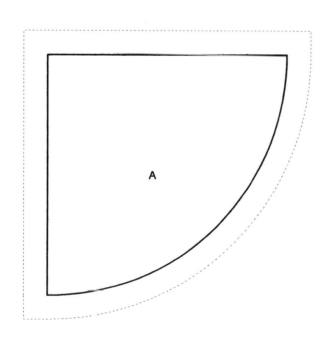

Template

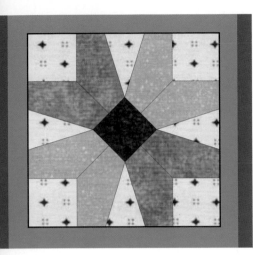

Little Boy's Britches

Block Size: 12" finished

Fabric Needed:

Cream shirting for background

Medium blue (denim color)

Light blue (chambray color)

Dark blue

This block also ran as Little Boy's Breeches in 1934.

We will use templates for this block.

Cutting Directions

From the shirting fabric, cut

4 squares using template A

4 triangles using template C

From the medium blue fabric, cut

2 pieces using template D

2 pieces using template B

From the light blue fabric, cut

2 pieces using template D

2 pieces using template B

From the dark blue fabric, cut

1 square using template E

To Make the Block

1 Sew the medium blue B and D pieces together.

2 Inset the A square.

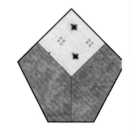

3 Add a C triangle to either side as shown. Make two units like this.

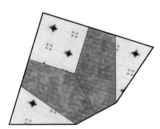

4 Stitch the light blue B and D pieces together.

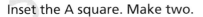

Inset the A square. Make two.

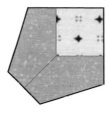

Sew the light blue units to the center square as shown.

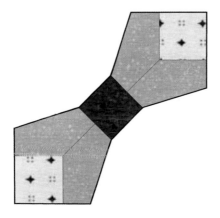

Inset the A square. Make two.

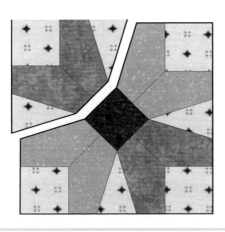

From The Kansas City Star,

September 6, 1939 :

No. 590

Original block - 9" pieced. Aside from the fact that this pattern is a relatively easy one to put together, it is a design in which print and 1-tone materials are effectively combined. The pattern was sent to The Weekly Star by Miss Hazel Brinley, Hillsboro, Mo.

From The Kansas City Star,

April 23, 1947:

No. 799

Original block – 9" pieced. This is a pattern in which both piecing and setting together of individual blocks are easily accomplished. The key to pleasing effectiveness is to alternate dark with light pieces, with the dark being preferably print and the light in one tone.

From The Kansas City Star,

July 16, 1938:

No. 554

Original block – 9" pieced. Here is an old pattern which has taken on new lines and an engaging new name, "Little Boy's Breeches," from the design which may be in blue on white.

The pattern also ran three times
as Little Boy's Breeches

From The Kansas City Star,

March 31, 1934:

No. 347

Original block – 9" pieced. The Little Boy's Breeches quilt pattern is a native Missourian, having been contributed to The Star by Mrs. J. H. Tine of Chaonia, Mo. The dark pieces and light pieces are combined in an interesting wheel arrangement. Allow for seams.

From The Kansas City Star,

May 17, 1961:

No. 1061

Original block – 9" pieced. For any boy's room this quilt of pieced Little Boy's Breeches would be very appropriate. The simple design comes from Mrs. Frank Stuever, 512 Central Street, Wichita 3.

"Plaid Britches" owned by Deb Rowden, Lawrence, Kansas. Designer unknown. Quilted by Lori Kukuk, McLouth, Kansas

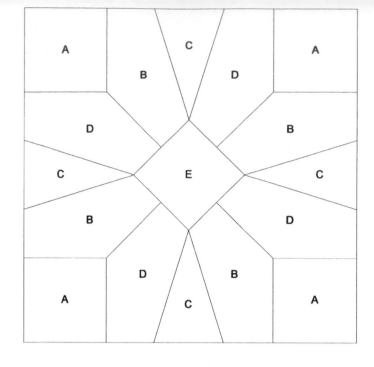

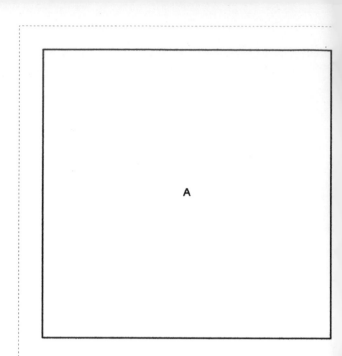

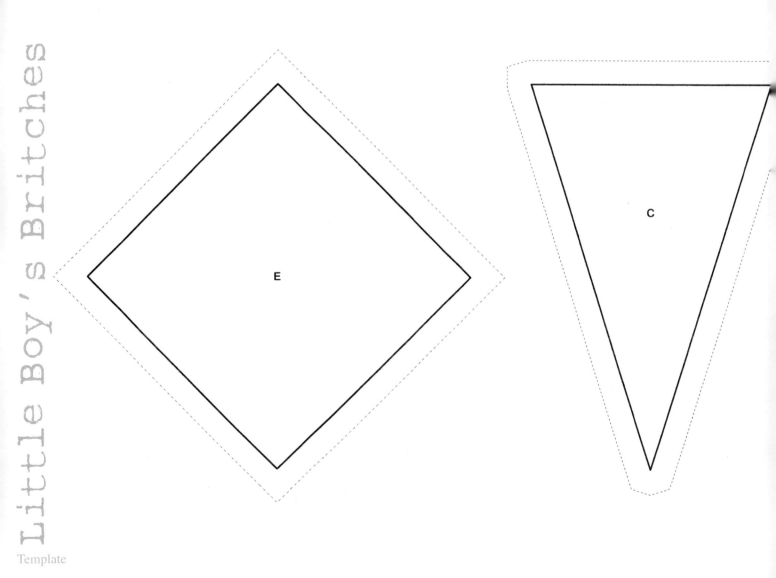

Little Boy's Britches

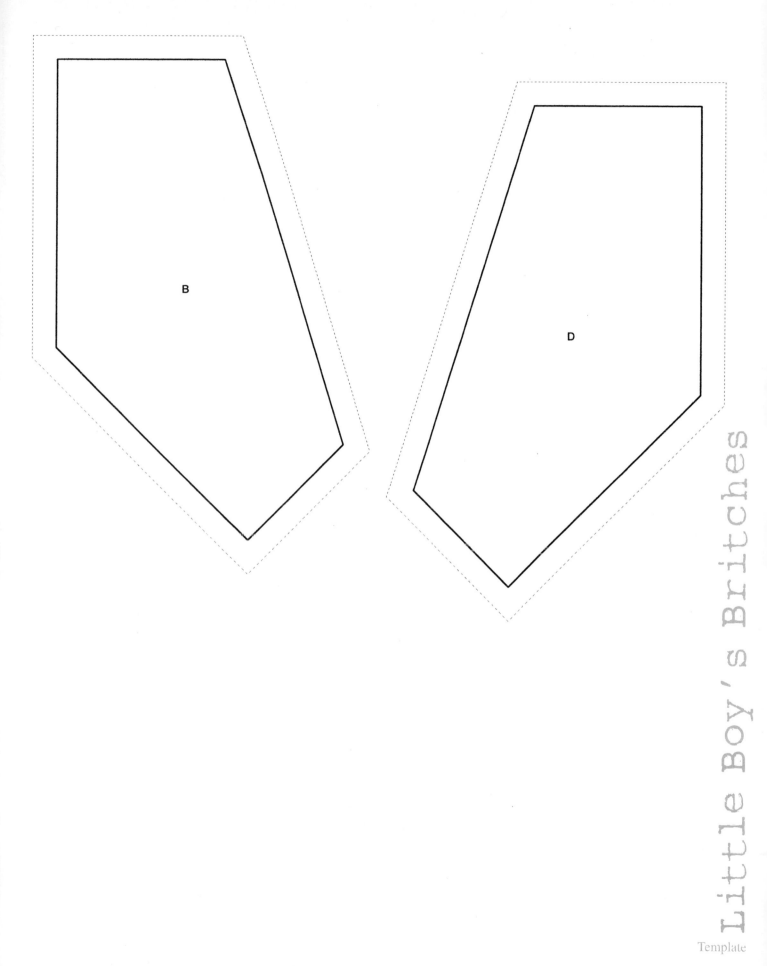

B

D

Little Boy's Britches

Template

Other Kansas City Star Quilts Books

One Piece at a Time by Kansas City Star Books – 1999

More Kansas City Star Quilts by Kansas City Star Books – 2000

Outside the Box: Hexagon Patterns from The Kansas City Star by Edie McGinnis – 2001

Prairie Flower: A Year on the Plains by Barbara Brackman – 2001

The Sister Blocks by Edie McGinnis – 2001

Kansas City Quiltmakers by Doug Worgul – 2001

O' Glory: Americana Quilt Blocks from The Kansas City Star by Edie McGinnis – 2001

Hearts and Flowers: Hand Appliqué from Start to Finish by Kathy Delaney – 2002

Roads and Curves Ahead: A Trip Through Time with Classic Kansas City Star *Quilt Blocks* by Edie McGinnis – 2002

Celebration of American Life: Appliqué Patterns Honoring a Nation and Its People by Barb Adams and Alma Allen – 2002

Women of Grace & Charm: A Quilting Tribute to the Women *Who Served in World War II* by Barb Adams and Alma Allen – 2003

A Heartland Album: More Techniques in Hand Appliqué by Kathy Delaney – 2003

Quilting a Poem: Designs Inspired by America's Poets by Frances Kite and Deb Rowden – 2003

Carolyn's Paper Pieced Garden: Patterns for Miniature and Full-Sized Quilts by Carolyn Cullinan McCormick – 2003

Friendships in Bloom: Round Robin Quilts by Marjorie Nelson and Rebecca Nelson-Zerfas – 2003

Baskets of Treasures: Designs Inspired by Life Along the River by Edie McGinnis – 2003

Heart & Home: Unique American Women and the Houses that Inspire by Kathy Schmitz – 2003

Women of Design: Quilts in the Newspaper by Barbara Brackman – 2004

The Basics: An Easy Guide to Beginning Quiltmaking by Kathy Delaney – 2004

Four Block Quilts: Echoes of History, Pieced Boldly & Appliquéd Freely by Terry Clothier Thompson – 2004

No Boundaries: Bringing Your Fabric Over the Edge by Edie McGinnis – 2004

Horn of Plenty for a New Century by Kathy Delaney – 2004

Quilting the Garden by Barb Adams and Alma Allen – 2004

Stars All Around Us: Quilts and Projects Inspired by a Beloved Symbol by Cherie Ralston – 2005

Quilters' Stories: Collecting History in the Heart of America by Deb Rowden – 2005

Libertyville: Where Liberty Dwells, There is My Country by Terry Clothier Thompson – 2005

Sparkling Jewels, Pearls of Wisdom by Edie McGinnis – 2005

Grapefruit Juice and Sugar: Bold Quilts Inspired by Grandmother's Legacy by Jenifer Dick – 2005

Home Sweet Home by Barb Adams and Alma Allen – 2005

Patterns of History: The Challenge Winners by Kathy Delaney – 2005

My Quilt Stories by Debra Rowden – 2005

Quilts in Red and Green and the Women Who Made Them by Nancy Hornback and Terry Clothier Thompson – 2006

Hard Times, Splendid Quilts: A 1930s Celebration, Paper Piecing from The Kansas City Star by Carolyn Cullinan McCormick – 2006

Art Nouveau Quilts for the 21st Century by Bea Oglesby – 2006

Designer Quilts: Great Projects from Moda's Best Fabric Artists – 2006

Birds of a Feather by Barb Adams and Alma Allen – 2006

Feedsacks! Beautiful Quilts from Humble Beginnings by Edie McGinnis – 2006

Kansas Spirit: Historical Quilt Blocks and the Saga of the Sunflower State by Jeanne Poore – 2006

Bold Improvisation: Searching for African-American Quilts – The Heffley Collection by Scott Heffley – 2007

The Soulful Art of African-American Quilts: Nineteen Bold, Improvisational Projects by Sonie Ruffin – 2007

Alphabet Quilts: Letters for All Ages by Bea Oglesby – 2007

Beyond the Basics: A Potpourri of Quiltmaking Techniques by Kathy Delaney – 2007

Golden's Journal: 20 Sampler Blocks Honoring Prairie Farm Life by Christina DeArmond, Eula Lang and Kaye Spitzli – 2007

Borderland in Butternut and Blue: A Sampler Quilt to Recall the Civil War Along the Kansas/Missouri Border by Barbara Brackman – 2007

Come to the Fair: Quilts that Celebrate State Fair Traditions by Edie McGinnis – 2007

Cotton and Wool: Miss Jump's Farewell by Linda Brannock – 2007

You're Invited! Quilts and Homes to Inspire by Barb Adams and Alma Allen of Blackbird Designs – 2007

Portable Patchwork: Who Says You Can't Take it With You? by Donna Thomas – 2008

Quilts for Rosie: Paper Piecing Patterns from the '40s by Carolyn Cullinan McCormick – 2008

Fruit Salad: Appliqué Designs for Delicious Quilts by Bea Oglesby – 2008

Red, Green and Beyond by Nancy Hornback and Terry Clothier Thompson – 2008

A Dusty Garden Grows by Terry Clothier Thompson – 2008

We Gather Together: A Harvest of Quilts by Jan Patek – 2008

With These Hands: 19th Century-Inspired Primitive Projects for Your Home by Maggie Bonanomi – 2008

As the Cold Wind Blows by Barb Adams and Alma Allen of Blackbird Designs – 2008

Caring for Your Quilts: Textile Conservation, Repair and Storage by Hallye Bone – 2008

The Circuit Rider's Quilt: An Album Quilt Honoring a Beloved Minister by Jenifer Dick – 2008

Embroidered Quilts: From Hands and Hearts by Christina DeArmond, Eula Lang and Kaye Spitzli – 2008

Reminiscing: A Whimsicals Collection by Terri Degenkolb – 2008

Scraps and Shirttails: Reuse, Re-purpose and Recycle! The Art of Green Quilting by Bonnie Hunter – 2008

Flora Botanica: Quilts from the Spencer Museum of Art by Barbara Brackman – 2009

Making Memories: Simple Quilts from Cherished Clothing by Deb Rowden – 2009

Pots de Fleurs: A Garden of Applique Techniques by Kathy Delaney – 2009

Wedding Ring, Pickle Dish and More: Paper Piecing Curves by Carolyn McCormick – 2009

The Graceful Garden: A Jacobean Fantasy Quilt by Denise Sheehan – 2009

My Stars: Patterns from The Kansas City Star, Volume I – 2009

Opening Day: 14 Quilts Celebrating the Life and Times of Negro Leagues Baseball by Sonie Ruffin – 2009

St. Louis Stars: Nine Unique Quilts that Spark by Toby Lischko – 2009

Whimsyland: Be Cre8ive with Lizzie B by Liz & Beth Hawkins – 2009

Cradle to Cradle by Barbara Jones of Quilt Soup – 2009

Pick of the Seasons: Quilts to Inspire You Through the Year by Tammy Johnson and Avis Shirer of Joined at the Hip – 2009

Across the Pond: Projects Inspired by Quilts of the British Isles by Bettina Havig – 2009

Artful Bras: Hooters, Melons and Boobs, Oh My! A Quilt Guild's Fight Against Breast Cancer by the Quilters of South Carolina - 2009

Flags of the American Revolution by Jan Patek – 2009

Get Your Stitch on Route 66: Quilts from the Mother Road by Christina DeArmond, Eula Lang and Kaye Spitzli from Of One Mind – 2009

Gone to Texas: Quilts from a Pioneer Woman's Journals by Betsy Chutchian – 2009

Juniper and Mistletoe: A Forest of Applique by Karla Menaugh and Barbara Brackman - 2009

My Stars II: Patterns from The Kansas City Star, Volume II – 2009

Nature's Offerings: Primitive Projects Inspired by the Four Seasons by Maggie Bonanomi – 2009

Quilts of the Golden West: Mining the History of the Gold and Silver Rush by Cindy Brick – 2009

Women of Influence: 12 Leaders of the Suffrage Movement by Sarah Maxwell and Dolores Smith of Homestead Hearth– 2009

Adventures with Leaders and Enders: Make More Quilts in Less Time! by Bonnie Hunter – 2010

A Bird in Hand: Folk Art Projects Inspired by Our Feathered Friends by Renee Plains – 2010

Feedsack Secrets: Fashion from Hard Times by Gloria Nixon – 2010

Greetings from Tucsadelphia: Travel-Inspired Projects from Lizzie B Cre8ive by Liz & Beth Hawkins – 2010

The Big Book of Bobbins: Fun, Quilty Cartoons by Julia Icenogle – 2010

Country Inn by Barb Adams and Alma Allen of Blackbird Designs – 2010

My Stars III: Patterns from The Kansas City Star, Volume III – 2010

Piecing the Past: Vintage Quilts Recreated by Kansas Troubles by Lynne Hagmeier – 2010

Stitched Together: Fresh Projects and Ideas for Group Quilting by Jill Finley – 2010

A Case for Adventures by Katie Kerr – 2010

A Little Porch Time: Quilts with a Touch of Southern Hospitality by Lynda Hall – 2010

Circles: Floral Applique in the Round by Bea Oglesby – 2010

Comfort Zone: More Primitive Projects for You and Your Home by Maggie Bonanomi – 2010

Leaving Baltimore: A Prairie Album Quilt by Christina DeArmond, Eula Lang and Kaye Spitzli from Of One Mind – 2010

Like Mother, Like Daughter: Two Generations of Quilts by Karen Witt and Erin Witt – 2010

Sew Into Sports: Quilts for the Fans in Your Life by Barbara Brackman – 2010

Under the Stars by Cherie Ralston – 2010

A Path to the Civil War: Aurelia's Journey Quilt by Sarah Maxwell and Dolores Smith of Homestead Hearth – 2010

Across the Wide Missouri: A Quilt Reflecting Life on the Frontier by Edie McGinnis and Jan Patek – 2010

Cottage Charm: Cozy Quilts and Cross Stitch Projects by Dawn Heese – 2010

My Stars IV: Patterns from The Kansas City Star, Volume IV – 2010

Roaring Through the 20s: Paper Pieced Quilts from the Flapper Era by Carolyn Cullinan McCormick – 2010

Project Books:

Fan Quilt Memories by Jeanne Poore – 2000

Santa's Parade of Nursery Rhymes by Jeanne Poore – 2001

As the Crow Flies by Edie McGinnis – 2007

Sweet Inspirations by Pam Manning – 2007

Quilts Through the Camera's Eye by Terry Clothier Thompson – 2007

Louisa May Alcott: Quilts of Her Life, Her Work, Her Heart by Terry Clothier Thompson – 2008

The Lincoln Museum Quilt: A Reproduction for Abe's Frontier Cabin by Barbara Brackman and Deb Rowden – 2008

Dinosaurs - Stomp, Chomp and Roar by Pam Manning – 2008

Carrie Hall's Sampler: Favorite Blocks from a Classic Pattern Collection by Barbara Brackman – 2008

Just Desserts: Quick Quilts Using Pre-cut Fabrics by Edie McGinnis – 2009

Christmas at Home: Quilts for Your Holiday Traditions by Christina DeArmond, Eula Lang and Kaye Spitzli from Of One Mind - 2009

Geese in the Rose Garden by Dawn Heese – 2009

Winter Trees by Jane Kennedy – 2009

Ruby Red Dots: Fanciful Circle-Inspired Designs by Sheri M. Howard – 2009

Backyard Blooms: A Month by Month Garden Sampler by Barbara Jones of QuiltSoup – 2010

Not Your Grandmother's Quilt: An Applique Twist on Traditional Pieced Blocks by Sheri M. Howard – 2010

A Second Helping of Desserts: More Sweet Quilts Using Pre-cut Fabric by Edie McGinnis – 2010

Café au Lait: Paper Piece a Rocky Road to Kansas by Edie McGinnis – 2010

Border Garden by Lynne Hagmeier – 2010

From the Bedroom to the Barnyard: A 9-Block Sampler Honoring Barn Quilts – 2010

Picnic Park by Barbara Jones of QuiltSoup – 2010

Hot Off the Press Patterns

Cabin in the Stars by Jan Patek – 2009

Arts & Crafts Sunflower by Barbara Brackman – 2009

Birthday Cake by Barbara Brackman – 2009

Strawberry Thief by Barbara Brackman – 2009

French Wrens by Dawn Heese - 2010

Queen Bees Mysteries:

Murders on Elderberry Road by Sally Goldenbaum – 2003

A Murder of Taste by Sally Goldenbaum – 2004

Murder on a Starry Night by Sally Goldenbaum – 2005

Dog-Gone Murder by Marnette Falley – 2008

DVD Projects:

The Kansas City Stars: A Quilting Legacy – 2008